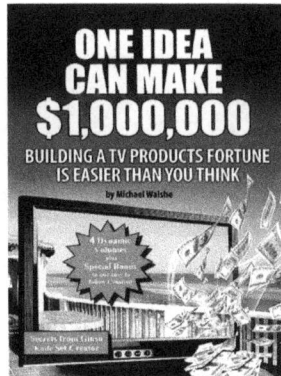

One Idea Can Make $1,000,000

Building a TV products fortune is easier than you think!

Michael Walshe

Published by:
Sales Magic, Inc.
2107 Corporate Drive
Boynton Beach
Florida 33426

E Mail: Michael@MichaelWalshe.com

Michael Walshe's list of TV product money spinners is the track record of an expert...

Ginsu Knife - Miracle Painter - Miracle Slicer - Armourcote Cookware Chinese Wok and Steamer - Shur Lok Wrench Set - Easy Iron
Power Driver - Network Watches - Maestro Pen Set   Eversharp Saw Space Maker Closet Organizer - Rocket Chef - Titanium II Knife Set
Family Name Origin & Meaning

You can now learn from - and be helped by - this world class expert....

You can read more about the author at the end of these books. Knowing about the man behind the secrets and his experience can be important as you use the teachings you will now study. But first of all this must be about YOU.

Michael Walshe will not take second best – and insists on you going forward to realize your own dreams and do it with vigor and vitality. He does not take NO for an answer and neither should you.

Go to the first page right away....

4 Volumes....
This work was created in 4 distinct volumes in order to address very clearly what you will need to find and develop a product - plus get it into the "As Seen On TV" business. For your convenience all 4 volumes have now been merged into a single book contained in 1 cover.

Volume 1

One Idea Can Make $1,000,000

Introduction

Start right now….
No delay – no excuses, just do it!

One idea can make $1,000,000 and I speak from experience. What you will read is more than a lesson – it comes from a lifetime of knowledge and I have been working on these writings, one way or another, for many years.

Don't look in these pages for a huge volume of information that will take you months to read and maybe longer to understand. You don't want an enormous amount of "fluff" designed simply to fill a book with words you may never read - and I don't want to write like that. Simply put, I want you to succeed and I have kept my writing deliberately short so that it is not difficult for you to form a succinct plan to go forward, right away. To start on a project that can produce success for you. I want to present logic, from over 45 years of experience, that you can follow and learn quickly and easily. What I am providing is expertise, not overbearing, complicated writings. What I have written is short, to the point and all you need to know to get started in the big money industry of Direct Response TV – also known as DRTV.

Don't forget that when you have your product I am ready to do an evaluation for you. This includes tips on bonus products, and the sequence to present them in a TV commercial. There is no rush to do this now as you can get in touch when your product is ready. At that time simply complete the Product Outline at the end of my book titled "The Easy Way To Finance" and e mail it to the address shown. You can also use this Product Outline for an effective proposal to product promoters – companies in the DRTV business.

By the way, you may wonder why I have put the information in separate books when it could easily be included in just one. The reason is simple – I want to make it easy for you to focus on the distinct areas of the DRTV business and learn that each area is important in its own right. I also believe this will help you form a logical step-by-step plan.

This is not a biography or an overview of my career. Sure, writings like that are interesting, and there are points to discover, but can you learn from them in a detailed manner? What I have written for you is a precise "how to" of ways to find products and ideas and develop them into TV winners. You will learn how to brand these products and deal with promoters in order to raise finance and get them on the air. Most important, you will find out about the elements that go into making a successful TV product.

I've said it can be easy and it can – and, here's the important part; you must provide the winning element in that you must focus. Don't try to do everything at once, just find a direction that suits you and go for it. Don't take months preparing but go forward and learn more as you go – if you make mistakes correct them. You don't have to do it all alone – as you will see, there is help, and resources, available in various ways. Above all, stick to it - do not give up.

It all starts with a product. You'll hear many times that the "product is king" and it is. But the demonstration (the pitch) is the "supporter" that elevates the "king" on high. So, the logical place to start is to get you on the quest for a great product – THE product that can change your life. If you find the demonstration to go with the product, all the better. Maybe you can learn enough to create your own powerful demonstration. Watch some of the demonstrators, or pitchmen, and you will learn. Always be on the lookout for that bit of "magic" that is the "hallmark" of all good Direct Response TV items.

Motivation – If You Need Some – Let's Get it Right Up Front!

Of course we all need to enjoy what we are doing but it's a known fact that getting money also tends to motivate most people. I said that I would give details of some payments my businesses have received in connection with developing products and TV presentations to go with them. These are real payments from real companies and the details are from the original checks.

Here are some examples showing details of the actual Paying Companies and Amounts:

Best Direct (International), Ltd. - $82,546.36

Best Direct (International), Ltd. - $112,355.90

Best Direct (International), Ltd. - $39,251.40

Best Direct (International), Ltd. - $42,158.63

Best Direct (International), Ltd. - $71,710.20

Best Direct (International), Ltd. - $77,284.30

QVC, Inc. - $211,020.72

QVC, Inc. - $380,400.83

QVC, Inc. - $638,569.94

QVC, Inc. - $665,508,86

QVC, Inc. - $875,612.43

QVC, Inc. - $1,002,152.88

Can you get checks like this? Like I said, I'm just a regular guy. Now read all my books.

Summary

Read all these pages to find out:

How to find a winning product – How to brand your product – How to get your product financed – How to identify, and develop, a winning product – My own "Million Dollar" secret.

Many times, in this industry, you'll hear statements like: "We're not in the business of selling dozens or hundreds, but millions when we can"

Maybe you already have a product or idea – OK, still read these pages and start right now to help you figure out the direction to take and how to go about it.

Right now, the most important part is getting started – do it now!

Michael Walshe

Read all the way through. My own "Million Dollar" secret! Is contained in these pages. Be on the lookout for it.

Bright Ideas.......

Bright ideas are all around you - everywhere you go. All you need to do is put yourself in the right mental state to notice them. Set your focus to always be on the lookout for a best selling product and be constantly observant. At first you may have to concentrate and train yourself to do this but after a while it will become second nature to you.

Here are a list of the places you are likely to discover bright ideas:

* **Home Shows and other Public Exhibitions**
* **State Fairs and County Fairs**
* **Craft Shows**
* **Festivals**
* **Flea Markets**
* **Street Markets**
* **Trade Shows**
* **Invention Shows**
* **Department & Discount Stores**
* **Mail Order Catalogs**
* **Newspapers and Magazines**
* **T.V. Programs**
* **TV Shopping Channels**
* **Schools, Colleges & Universities**
* **YouTube**
* **Business and Product TV Shows**
* **Internet and Search Engines**

We will examine them one at a time because all of these areas can be a source of bright ideas that fall into various categories such as:

* **New products** that have come to the market without much fanfare. Many times they have not been positioned or promoted in the most desirable way and can be positioned to attract attention. You'll find them on store shelves, displayed with their own category, hardware, cleaning items or whatever. Look for very basic packaging as this is often a clue to a low budget marketing approach. The secret is to look for something you don't instantly

recognize as this indicates it may not have been advertised widely. If you determine that the item has features and benefits which can be portrayed in an effective demonstration, and that the it enjoys some of the other aspects which determine the profile of a best selling product, purchase a sample immediately and go to work on it. Sit down and start to create a demonstration, think about positioning, a sales concept and a dynamic brand name.

* **Old products** which can be revived or positioned in a new way. You will take most of the same approach outlined above in regard to new products. The packaging may be fancy and the item may have been extensively advertised many years before but now it is ready for revival. New generations of consumers come along, people get married and start families, they move into new homes and so on. The requirement for the same products starts all over again.   The key to look for is can the item fill a need or be the solution to a problem.

* **Sleepers,** these are products which have probably been launched on a limited budget, usually in a "grass roots" type of fashion, but have the elements of a winning item. Look for all the same clues outlined above. Think of yourself as prospector or a detective, both of these people look for clues in their quest which will lead them to the target - you will be doing essentially the same thing, playing the same role. Sometimes items like this can be produced relatively easily or you may be able to approach the manufacturer and advise them that you have a way to sell the product in huge volume.

* **Demonstration products** that have not yet been exposed to TV advertising. In particular you should look for those which, although they could be, are not actually being demonstrated or where the demonstration is somewhat basic and unpolished, even crude.   These are usually items just starting out and the person promoting them has not yet created an effective demonstration. Eventually all the sales points and unique selling benefits will be molded into an effective and perhaps dynamic presentation.   This is

the point where most TV promotion companies discover this type of item because by then it should be blatantly obvious. But not always, and many miss the obvious so don't ignore those demonstrators with highly polished approach, the key is to find out if the product is already been shown on Tand if it has been successful. You are primarily looking for items that have not as yet had media exposure. By finding an item which has demonstration capability but where the final sales approach has not yet been worked out you will be getting in on the first rung of the ladder, so move fast because someone else soon will. A word about demonstration products which have been shown on TV with no success, don't ignore them as many times a second stab has been taken at an item. This has produced winners from previous failures and winners from previously so-so items. New positioning, a revamped package of items including more dramatic bonuses, a new approach to the TV commercial, these are just some of the ways to turn a loser into a winner.

* Now let us take a closer look at the places where you are likely to find winners:

Home Shows and other public exhibitions.

These can be Home Shows, State & County Fairs, Town & City Shows (local community events), Auto Shows, Boat Shows – they can be exhibitions for crafts, food, flowers, fitness, DIY - and virtually any category that the general public finds interesting.
What to look for and how to do it? The methods are very similar at a variety of different events. Here is an overview of the main events, what to expect and what to do.

These events are probably the best source of winning products and many high profile all time best sellers had their roots in this type of environment.

At Home Shows, demonstrators abound at display booths they refer to as "joints". Their dynamic and often colorful demonstrations can be motivating and inspiring, these presentations are at all times captivating for this is the essence of successful selling. After all, a direct response TV commercial or infomercial is in effect a demonstration that has been adapted to suit the electronic media. To be successful the TV spot must contain at least the major elements of the demonstration, follow an equally logical sequence and contain what I call the "magic factor" – a dramatic part of the demo that really excites you and illustrates a benefit that makes the product so very special. In this last sentence you have the true secret of how to look for winning demonstration items that can be turned in to best seller TV products, note it down and remember it well. If you are working on a demonstration for a product just ask yourself this; "If I had the power what would I make this product do?" Then see if the product can do it. That's how you find the most dramatic elements of a demonstration. Now with all this talk about demonstrations do not ignore those products without polished presentations. Those with perhaps a basic, un-flowing, "how-to" type of demonstration. By using "how-to" in this context what I mean is you should look for the guy who is simply showing the benefits of a product in an "it does this and you can make it do that", almost instructional, type of way. The reason for this is that the item is new and the demonstrator has not as yet added stories and examples to the basic elements of the product, that's the next stage in creating the demonstration or "pitch", and then it has to be made to flow just like any good story or speech for instance. I remember going to a flower show way out in the country some years ago and finding a friend of mine on his first day out to demonstrate a new item. He had been guarding this product with great secrecy and was amazed to see me turn up right on his first day out, particularly as I had traveled about five thousand miles to be there. Now this man is a world leader in his field but like all of us in the business he had to start out with a basic demonstration for this new product, which he would then take several months to hone, perfect and polish into a dynamic pitch. Well, I watched him present the item to a crowd of people for about three demonstrations before I said, "can I have a go". More by luck than expertise I was fortunate enough to sell the very first one in the history of this item that went on to be demonstrated in quite a few countries. This became a landmark in my friendship with this product creator, although not the first one, which led to an ongoing mutual respect. So what does this story tell you? First it tells about a new product without, as yet, an effective sales approach. Second it tells you that many people use the type of event described to test the market for this type of item. Last but not least it shows that people who are highly qualified in the art of product development and marketing can, just as much as the new entrepreneur, be found trying out their merchandise in small shows, large exhibitions and even in flea markets or street markets. You must literally dig around and explore every nook and cranny of these events and believe me when I say that the "joint" right at the back of the show, tucked around a corner, with nobody   paying much attention to it, could be hiding the next big TV winner. Why? Because there's a person there who is new to the business, with a product that's never been seen, but that person can't get a good location in the show because all the prime spots are booked from year to year by established players in the game. Here's a simple system for exploring the show to scout for products:

1. Walk the show and look at all items that are being demonstrated. This includes unpolished presentations that can be made into a demo. In fact, look at any item that you think a demonstration can be applied to.
2. Take careful note of the demonstrations – write down their exact sequence. Look (and listen) to see what problem the item solves. Note if the main benefit comes early in the demonstration.

3. On your way out stop and take a few moments to grade the products you have noted. Make and league table starting at the one you think is best and so on down.

4. When you get home, screen out those items that are already being advertised, currently, on TV. You are looking for products that do not already have mass exposure. Even though you may have spent time looking at products, and taking notes about items that you will not use, this is time well spent. You will be in training to improve you product, and demonstration, selection skills.

State Fairs and County Fairs

The same guidelines apply as for Home Shows but usually you will have a lot more ground to cover.   State and County Fairs are spread out over a wide area covering many acres and displaying an enormous amount of merchandise. The new guys, those with, as yet, unproven products tend to be housed together in a remote part of the showgrounds.   This is good because you can find many opportunities under one roof.   Go to this section first; take along a small cassette tape player to note down the demonstration – include a sequence of the visual actions together with a rough out of the words - and to take your own notes. Remember this recording is only an audio portion, the actions related to the product together with the sequence of the presentation are also important. So after watching the demonstration walk away from the booth, tell your recorder the name of the product, and while it's fresh in your mind relate the actions in the sequence they happened. Of course you can also take notes but recording is easier and less cumbersome when on the move in a busy show.   After visiting this section of the show go to the buildings or outside areas where you can find the established demonstrators show their wares. Now you will be looking for those products that have not been shown on TV. Sometimes these items may have been around for a while but nobody has discovered their full potential. Perhaps you can think of a new way to position an item, a unique selling concept or a way to package it with others (look for dynamic bonuses) that are compatible with it to create what is known as a "lump up".   These lump ups have been some of the enormous winners of all times..... remember the Ginsu Knife Set?.... who could forget it? Lump up packages, which are basically a kit or set of products with a common theme or compatibility, rely also on giving dramatic bonus items along with the offer, these are known as "bung ons" – or bonuses. "Order now and we'll include this amazing slicer-dicer.... it chops... it slices and is guaranteed to cure all the world's problems in the first five minutes of use".... you get the idea.   Well these bung ons, and we'll get into them some more in other parts of my writing, must be star items in their own right.

It is no good throwing in something that is just in itself a cheap item with no dramatic appeal.   Bung ons must project value but at the same time give the offer an appeal that is out of proportion to their cost.   The spiral slicer in the original Ginsu offer did just that. It cost about sixteen cents yet it was a unique and intriguing item that got many people to the phone to order the package. These bonuses could never be the top billing star in a package because on their own they could not command a high enough price point to make an offer economically viable but believe me when I say they could make the difference between a sale or no sale.   The object of me telling you all this is to ensure that you look at every potential product in two ways.... one as the main item for a package or to sell on its own.... and also to be on the look out for bonus items. They may not suit a project you are currently working on but can come in useful at a future time, so keep good notes and store the information away.   Make sure you look everywhere so as not to miss that potential winner. Some products may not be demonstrated in any way, so don't imagine you should just look at the "pitch men" only. You could easily find an item just lying on a counter or a shelf yet it may have features that could be demonstrated and form the makings of a compelling TV commercial.

Craft Shows

These are often a treasure chest of innovation, as every booth will house a creative person. Among the many home made items you could find a new toy or gimmick item. So-called fad items, for instance, can have vast appeal and become tremendously popular within a short space of time. Remember the yo-yo, the hula-hoop, the pet rock and more recently the beanie babies?   I had an item years ago that was called the Lunar Zoomer, when you swung it around your head wind rushed through it and created a sound that was like a tune from outer space, not that I've ever actually heard a tune in outer space but imagination is a wonderful coach. This gimmick was loved by kids and was easily made too. All I needed was some flexible extruded plastic piping that was formed so that it had a corrugated look, this piping was cut into lengths of approximately thirty inches and they were ready to sell. I advertised in a trade paper to sell them, my niece and nephew appeared in a photo, demonstrating them and another gimmick product called the Clackers, which was placed in a write up alongside the ad, and my phone rang off the hook with callers wanting to place orders. We couldn't keep up with the demand but that's a nice problem to have. My nephew, who was kid at the time, grew up to be a rising star in the Direct Response TV business and maybe this early start gave him a taste for the game, but that's another story. Most times the products you find at craft shows will need a little creative development to polish them up for sale at the regular retail level. Not all will be suitable for TV selling but may be just the ticket for mail order print advertising or for launching directly into the retail store arena. Having said that, some toy items could be very successful as direct response TV items in the pre Christmas shopping season. So look at everything and perhaps eventually you will hit on a category that you have a knack for and you can focus on it.

Festivals

These may be festivals with a national or ethnic theme, or perhaps music or food festivals. Even renaissance festivals can be "pots of gold" for products and ideas. Look carefully as some of the ideas may go back centuries – can you adapt them to modern times? There are even balloon festivals and events of all kinds to cater for diverse interest groups, or just organized with the object of putting on a fun filled day for the family. The same rules as for Craft Shows apply here. Head for the craft section if there is one. If not dig around to see wherever there may be products for sales. Some of these events attract "fly pitchers", these are guys and gals who simply sell their wares anywhere there are people, at a show or festival or even in a busy street. They don't reserve space at the event, don't pay rent, and don't ask permission to sell their goods. They are however, for the person looking for new items, very useful, as they tend to be on the cutting edge when it comes to sourcing innovative and unique items. I met a friend of mine who is a fly pitcher at a festival a couple of years ago, he had a bag full of a product which he had found in England and wanted to see if it would be equally as popular in the USA.   It was a plastic item which when inflated formed the shape of a giant hammer.... kids, and adults who wanted to have the same fun as their kids, could go around bopping their friends on the head with this fake tool, without doing any damage but getting a huge laugh. This went on to be a popular fad item around the world. Now, don't get me wrong, I'm not suggesting this would be a good TV product – not at all. But you can find some great products being sold by fly pitchers. They work the streets of big cities like New York and London. Look for demonstration items and you may find something that the fly pitchers got before anyone else. What about the story of Joe Addes who sold a small vegetable slicer on the streets of New York. Joe got a lot of exposure on YouTube and was even featured on a national morning TV show. Now a similar item is a big TV products hit. I wonder if somebody saw Joe working it first.

Flea Markets, Swap Meets and Street Markets

I've put these together because the same guidelines, as to searching for products, apply to them.   Markets are the oldest vehicles for merchandising and selling and they go back many centuries, even to Biblical times. In the USA there are flea markets, sometimes called swap meets. In European countries they have street markets, many of which have been around since medieval times. This form of trading took place well before the advent of sophisticated stores or sales through the mass media. Selling products using demos started at street markets and town markets. Some of these markets go back many centuries in Europe. For this reason the market way of selling constitutes the very root and essence of product development and merchandising technique. I would urge all my readers to take some dedicated time to study markets and if you ever have the opportunity to visit Europe, take a couple of weeks and travel round some of these shopper paradises. I promise you that it will be an eye opener, an education and a thoroughly enjoyable experience all rolled into one.   Tour a market, and it is a tour as some of them can be vast, as you would a show or exhibition. Always be on the look out for folks who are selling their products in the streets – in England they are called "fly pitchers" and they are very innovative in finding products. They are constantly scouting and searching for clever ideas. If the market is in your local area go back every week or from time to time as you never know when new items will pop up, the marketplace is an ever-changing arena of intriguing merchandise. Always be on the lookout for demonstration products. Take along your tape recorder for getting the essence of demonstrations, and notes. Perhaps a camera to take some photos, even a video camera will come in useful. Be sure to write down the sequence, and flow, of a demonstration. Early on you should see how the item solves a problem – you should see the biggest benefits early in the demonstration. Where a market is different to a show is that a booth or stall may contain a variety of products some seemingly unrelated, on the other hand the joint may have a common theme. So take your time and dig around, talk to people and ask if there is anything new around, they may tell you and they may be secretive but you have noting to lose and may start a network of new friends and scouts. I have people from all over the world offering me products as a result of relationships I've built up over the years so you can do it too. You could even take a product on board and sell it at a market yourself, or work for someone in the business, this way you could really get into the swim of the game. Think about it because you could make money while you learn. Markets and shows truly are the universities of sales and marketing. A more recent concept in markets found in Europe is what are known as car boot sales. These are much like American flea markets or swap meets, even perhaps like a gathering of yard sales. People arrive in their cars, pay a small fee for the day's trading and sell right from the trunk, or boot, as it's known as - in some European countries - of their car. They may be selling new goods or just clearing out their house of what they consider to be rubbish. Well someone said that one persons rubbish (or trash) can be another's treasure and believe me this is very true. Like flea markets these boot sales can be a treasure trove of merchandise and even ideas for new products. You can sometimes find an old and used item that someone has had lying around the house for years, it may be long forgotten in the retail arena and ready for revival.... it may need updating for modern times, but it could be a great idea and a tremendous find. One of the prime resources at markets are the vendors who work there. They know, before anyone else, about what's doing well, hot new items and so on. So, talk to vendors and if it's a quiet time some will be only too glad to chat. If you find an unfriendly guy, then move on to the next. Be conversational, not to probing too strongly. People love to talk and you just need to steer the conversation towards new product. While I was doing some video taping in research for this piece a market vendor asked me what I was filming for, so I told him. Before long he was filling me with info and eventually I got his "whole life story" – all of our conversation was immensely interesting. As I've said elsewhere, many people go to a live selling environment in order to test market a new item and also to create selling techniques and demos. Focus groups and surveys are one thing but you can't beat the kind of feedback you get when people vote with their own money – by buying the product. The best thing about doing this kind of testing and research in a market is that a vendor space is about the most inexpensive retail spot to be found. Couple that with the available customer traffic and the fact that booking in advance is not usually required, anyone can just go to many markets, ask for a casual location for the day and they are in business - the situation is ideal for product testing and development. Just think about it somebody wants to try out a new product – they get the idea and within a few days they can be on a market, with as little as 50 to 100 pieces of the item, and ready to go. You could try it yourself and if you take some time to develop a demonstration, and try out some bonuses, you can build a better proposal to take you product to the next stage – to a TV products promoter.

Trade Shows

If you are fortunate enough to have these held in your own city or nearby please take advantage of them. They are an amazing source of new products of all kinds. You may have to travel to trade shows and conventions but if you are serious about getting into this business it will be well worth your time. Look for shows related to the major categories of items that sell well on TV, in print advertising or as hot items in retail stores. Housewares & home appliances, hardware, tools, DIY, craft items, automobile items, demonstration items, cleaners, sleeping helpers (including mattresses and toppers), fitness and slimming products, beauty and look good categories, weight loss, skin care & beauty, pain relief, vitamins and supplements, motivational & self improvement tapes, discs and books, business opportunities, hobby products, musical compilations, collectibles and heritage & ancestry are some of the main areas to look at. These shows are always laid out in an organized and easy to get around fashion but do allow time for the bigger ones so you are able to search and study carefully – and I do mean cover the whole show.   All trade shows have a directory, which you get when registering to enter, this serves as a good guide to the show and should be kept to use as an excellent source book for items you may be working on in the future. A word about registering which may save you time and trouble later. Most shows require attendees to be in the particular industry covered by the show or a related field. Make sure you have some notepaper and business cards with your company name or trading name. By writing to the show for registration forms in advance you can many times save yourself paying an entrance fee of as much as fifty dollars or more plus you will save yourself the time of lining up to register, sometimes thirty minutes or more at a busy show. Of course, most times, you can also pre-register on the Internet – simply find the show's website and you're on your way easily. You can, of course, register at the event but do make sure you have a business card to show at the registration booth. You'll also need an ample supply of these to hand out to exhibitors whose products you are interested in, they will be happy to give you literature or mail it on later.   Anyone you approach will want to know what business you are in so be sure to tell them you are involved with the TV Direct Response industry, as everyone wants to get their item on TV and you will immediately get focused attention. You need to stay focused too as you a can easily become overwhelmed by the massive variety of merchandise on show. Study the criteria which identifies a winning product, you'll find it elsewhere in my writings, and it will help you to zero in on those items which can be of use to you. Don't worry if you spread your net a little wide though as you can always throw some fish back and this will be better than missing the prize of the catch. When you return home sort through the literature you have gathered, categorize it, and make up a short list of the best items that you want to follow through on. Incidentally you will need a bag or briefcase to carry sales brochures and literature in and for a multiple day show pack an extra bag or case to pack your literature in for the journey home. My garage is filled with bags and cases I've had to buy for this very purpose. Here is my simple system for walking trade shows in order to best use your time and energy:

1. If the show is in sections figure out which parts will be of most use to you. What categories of products are you looking for? Always get the show directory (or catalog) – this can be a great aid to exploring the show and a valuable sourcing tool later.

2. If there is a new products (or inventions) section be sure to visit it first.

3. As always, look for items that can be demonstrated – even though they are not being demonstrated at the trade show.

4. As you walk the show, get literature on products that interest you. Also, note the website where you can study later.

5. When you have walked the entire show, find somewhere quiet to study the literature you have collected. Grade the items and then go back to the booths for those products. For the most part (and depending on the show layout), starting with the favorite in your grading and so on. Speak to the people representing the company and find out more. If you can't get back to all the booths you can follow up on the web and by phone.

6. Here's a note to remember, always start with the booths of the smaller companies. These are the folks who are working on new products and may also have "sleepers" they have been promoting for years – but just haven't "hit the spot" as the old saying goes. I don't mean that you should entirely ignore the booths with displays from the big companies. They have some great products but they will already have some substantial exposure. However, these booths can be a

source of some terrific bonuses – put them in your notes for a future time when they can fit in well with a star product. Then, of course, what about their losing items – some have great products that were just not promoted in the right way. There's a well-known story of the company that had a sandwich toaster product and had spent big money on its development and promotion. But, they put it in retail stores as an item just lying on the shelves and it never sold in big numbers. The sandwich toaster needed demonstrating – in fact, a similar item had been demonstrated, and sold very successfully, in Europe. This company had a warehouse full of them – stored away for years gathering dust. Along comes a pitchman, finds the product, works out an effective demonstration, puts the sandwich toaster on TV and makes it a home run!

Invention Shows

Inventors are passionate about their creations. Many have years and years of there lives tied into a dream and they will never give up until they see it turned into the final product and brought to market. A walk round an invention show can be an amazing revelation that shows just how many really bright people are living among us. Look carefully at these items and do not dismiss any at first sight. Of course, there will be many that are outside your sphere of interest but what I am pointing out is that some products may need a little development – some tweaking. Look at an invention not always as what it is – but what it can be made to be or what it can show. Open your imagination fully and you may find some true gems. Don't forget that your goal is to turn an item into a TV product. Remember what I say about bonuses. What can you put with the invention to make a dynamic package suitable for TV selling? Could the invention be suitable as a bonus with another product? When I was given the project of turning the Rocket Chef food processor from a loser into a winner, I put the Fat Free Gourmet – a wonderful cooking pan - with it. I was able to demonstrate how to cook gourmet meals with less fat and less calories. This and some more "doctoring" to the infomercial made this product a tremendous success.

Always look at an invention not just for what it IS but also for what it CAN BE SHOWN TO DO. What clever demonstrations can be applied to it? There's an old saying - "You don't sell the steak – you sell the sizzle". Get out to those invention shows – great places to prospect for your big winner. Go online and you can find details of many.

Some shows are solely for the presentation of inventions. But you will also find that, sometimes, there are new invention sections at other trade shows – such as housewares and hardware shows.

As you get used to visiting invention shows there a way you can take your presence to the next level. Find out if you can book a room, or even a table at the shows, where inventors can visit with you in order to present their products. Then promote yourself to the show's inventors – handing out a simple flyer to each booth should do it. You can also do a version of this approach right in your own hometown. Just set up an open meeting where inventors can visit you. Set a time, date and place – the place can be anywhere, in an office, a hotel meeting room or wherever is convenient for people to get to. Then put out a press release and run some classified ads in newspapers and online advertising websites like Craig's List. Phone round the local media -TV, newspapers and radio - to get the word out. You can even put a notice on some free bulletin boards such as in your local supermarket. Track down some inventors in your area and phone round to invite them. There may be some inventor groups or clubs locally - get in touch and let them know of your open meeting. Let the inventors come along at any time, no need to make appointments unless some people want to, and see them one at a time. Let inventors make their own presentations but you need to be prepared to know what you are looking for - the various elements that can make a good TV product. Can it solve a problem, can it be demonstrated and so on. Be sure to read all the way through in order to study these important points. This is important, be sure to keep contact details of all the inventors you meet - these can be very bright people and a valuable resource. Stay in touch with them – make sure they send you info on new items and any other tips that may help you. If something interesting comes up, meet with them again and see their presentation. These folks are always thinking and working on new items.

Last, but not least, on the subject of new inventions. You can also find invention programs on TV. Do your homework and use search engines on the Internet to find them. Watch them, record them, study them and look for your winning product.

Stores

Department stores and more. All manner of stores can be a treasure trove of bright ideas. Don't think for one moment that just because an item has found its way to the retail level that there is not further opportunity for it. An existing product can give you an idea, you may think of ways to further develop it, you may want to make it part of a larger package of items, a set or a kit perhaps. Always remember that as you proceed you will require items to use as bonuses (bung ons) for other packages, so take your notes and store those good ideas away. File them away, list them carefully, and keep them in mind for the time that one or more of them will fit with a star product to give it that bit extra to push your product over the winning line. The Armourcote Cookware set, which I developed back in the 70's, was looked on by some people to be doomed to failure. Why? Because there were many cooking pans on store shelves and at very good prices. Our advertising message was not specifically directed to selling pans but to selling the surface that we called Armourcote to project an image of strength and ruggedness.   We demonstrated these pans in our TV commercial to show their non-stick capability, the approach was powerful and a million pans later the prophets of doom were more than convinced. Many times items you see on store shelves have been positioned wrongly and a new approach, perhaps an entirely new sales concept that wraps them in a fresh image, will attract the customers' attention. Once in a while the product you are looking for may be displayed among the TV products but may only have had minimal television exposure, the store merchandiser will have put the items in this area because they have an innovative look just like TV items. This points to a sense of vision on the part of the merchandisers. They are swimming in new products every day so their eye for an item should act as a good clue for you. The further clue to look for is "Have I seen this item on TV?" If you watch TV, which you must do if you are going to be in this business, you'll automatically notice the items that are getting mass exposure so that those which are not will stand out like the proverbial "nugget of gold". On the other hand, you may find products of interest to you displayed with their own category, like hardware, cleaning items, housewares, tools, DIY or in virtually any department or area of the store. Basic packaging is often a clue to a low budget marketing approach. Look for items you don't instantly recognize as this indicates they may not have been advertised widely. If an item has features and benefits that can be portrayed in an effective demonstration, and it has some of the other aspects that indicate that it could be a best selling product, purchase a sample immediately and go to work on it. Take it home, work on creating a demonstration, make notes relating to positioning, think up some rough ideas for a sales concept and write down all your ideas for a dynamic brand name so you can hone down this list later. While looking around stores always be on the look out for hidden treasures in the form of old products which can be revived or positioned in a new way. You will take most of the same approach outlined above in regard to new products. The packaging may be fancy and the item may have been extensively advertised many years before but now it is ready for revival. New generations of consumers come along, people get married and start families, they move into new homes and so on. The requirement for the same products starts all over again. The same problems are encountered and, once again, solutions are needed. NEVER FORGET THE TV PRODUCTS MANTRA: PROBLEM – SOLUTION / PROBLEM – SOLUTION. The key to look for is... "Can the item fill a need or be the solution to a problem?". Much of this I have said before and I repeat these points in order to stress just how important they are. Always.... always.... look for sleepers, these can lead to your "pot of gold". They may be products that have been launched on a limited budget, possibly in a "grass roots" type of fashion, but they have the elements of a winning item. Look for all the same clues that I have outlined above. Many items can be produced relatively easily or you may be able to approach an existing manufacturer of an item and advise them that you have a way to sell the product in huge volume.

Mail Order Catalogs

These are amazing source references, you should collect them eagerly and file them efficiently.   They can pay dividends time and time again. Get put on mailing lists for catalogs and collect old ones anywhere you can find them, as they can be a great source of products ready for revival. When I brought the Miracle Painter to American TV viewers back in 1976, remember the opening of a man in a tuxedo painting a swirl ceiling? It was a huge success. Over 10 years later it was revived as the Euro Painter to a whole new generation of viewers to become a success all over again. Look through mail order catalogs in the same way as you would dig around stores, exhibitions, flea markets or anywhere else but you'll do it in the comfort of your own home. Many of the items you find in these catalogs started their life at a trade show and professional buyers employed by the catalog company spent many hours sifting through a huge volume of products to find the best sellers for the valuable space on their pages. They may have made many trips to countries in the Orient, all the time searching and digging to bring their customers the best of the best. As these people tend to have an eye for innovation you will find some outstanding products on catalog pages. Catalogs, however, have an advantage over retail stores in that they can use artwork or photographs together with hard-hitting sales copy to sell the products. So you'll notice that many of the items found in catalogs never find their way on to retailers' shelves and only get exposure to mail order buyers, a significant yet limited segment of the overall buying population. This is where you can find sleepers that are suitable for TV. Look to see if you can combine compatible items into a powerful package. Look, as always, for good bonuses. See if advertising copy for a product can form the basis for a demonstration. Study the features and benefits to develop your own demonstration. Think of ways to adapt the product and the pitch to be more suitable for TV. Add bonuses to build the item into a powerful package (a "lump up") that forms a dramatic approach to TV viewers. Look for innovation, look for gimmicks, and never forget to look for bung ons (bonuses) as your fingers do the walking through the exciting pages in the world of catalogs. Of course, these days, you can do the same on the Internet by visiting the catalog companies' websites. Some like paper, some like the computer screen – the choice is yours entirely. TV home shopping shows can be used in the same way. You can find hot winners that sell out at the test stage, lots of potential bonus items and oldies that need revamping and reviving.

Newspapers and Magazines

Another terrific source of products. Look for items sole directly by mail order. Be sure to include the tabloids and inserts as well as regular newspapers. If ads for them appear with repetition that's a big indicator that they are successful. But look beyond the ads for products, inventions or ideas that may be mentioned in articles – and do be sure to look in all sections because you never know where the next winner may be hiding. If you can get newspapers and magazines (also mail order catalogs) from other countries do take advantage of using them too. Many times products appear in other countries first. My Mum used to send me ads from London and, for many years, I had them pasted in scrapbooks – thanks Mum! Study, above, what I have said about developing mail order catalog items into TV product packages – the same approaches apply here.

TV Programs

Yes, even while watching all manner of TV shows you can find ideas for products. In particular you should focus on craft shows, how to shows, home and garden programs, food shows, cooking shows, do it yourself programs and any show which uses, or has, a connection to products. Sometimes you may actually see an item that the presenter is using, it may be in basic form, it may be old and worn, but it may also form the basis of an idea for a product. Watch the job or project that is being presented and you may be able to develop a way to do it better, faster, easier. For instance, if a show host is doing a home decorating project using a basic item to achieve a desired effect this may give you an idea to create a more sophisticated and marketable product to do the same thing in an easier fashion and more efficiently.   Craft shows are great because they are designed to literally give away bright ideas. Where this can benefit you is that these shows tend to appeal to a relatively select audience and you can therefore take an idea you find, develop it, and present it to the masses. Maybe while watching you will see a craft project completed using basic items found around the home and everyday tools. It will be presented in a how-to, step by step fashion. Think to yourself, is this something that can appeal to a lot of people, could it get attention, is this show putting across something that others would like to make? Is there an item I can create demos for? Does it have the "magic" factor? If the answers to all these questions are "Yes", you may have found something interesting.   Now think further, could the same process being shown be used to create a variety of items? Are you starting to get my drift? Perhaps you can put the pieces together, materials or whatever, in a kit together with the tools to do the job.... and BINGO!!!! - Now, you have a new product. Please bear in mind that I am simply giving you an example of how TV shows can present you with ideas, and this is just one example, but you can use this methodology and relate it to many other instances. You must mentally "step outside the box" and think freely, not everything is possible but do not discount any idea until you have thought it through thoroughly.... even the most far fetched ideas can sometimes be stepping stones to great ideas.

TV Shopping Channels

TV home shopping channels can be a terrific source of products. You can find hot winners that sell out at the test stage, lots of potential bonus items and oldies that need revamping and reviving. But there are so many products that I suggest you narrow down your selections. Here are some guidelines:

1. Look for items that are being, or can be, demonstrated.

2. Screen out items that already have heavy exposure - somebody else is already winning with them.

3. Look for new items that you are seeing on the channel but that are not being sold in TV spots or infomercials.

4. Look at the sales figures for the product. This is usually shown at the bottom of the screen at some time during the sales presentation. Do the figures look impressive, considering the time of day, week, month and year the product is on the air?

5. See if a new item sells out or gets close to selling out, because obviously this is a strong indicator.

Always look for old demonstration products that you have not seen around for a while - there are many "evergreens" that cycle with new generations.

File away ideas for bonus items, list them carefully, and keep them in mind for the time that one or more of them will fit with a star product to give it that bit extra to push your product over the winning line.
Once again, study, above, what I have said about developing mail order catalog items into TV product packages – the same approaches apply here.

Schools, Colleges & Universities

Some schools, colleges and universities have programs where students develop businesses and new products. Find out what is on offer in your area and ask if you can hold an open meeting to find out what new products and developments are available. Students, at any age, can be surprisingly bright and innovative. You may be able to do licensing deals or get involved in partnerships or joint ventures to manufacture or market new products. This may be a source of the next million dollar item.

YouTube

YouTube and other online video sites can be a "goldmine" of ideas and products. Let me repeat what I wrote previously about Joe Addes, the guy who demonstrated vegetable slicers on the New York streets:

"What about the story of Joe Addes, who sold a small vegetable slicer on the streets of New York. Joe got a lot of exposure on YouTube and was even featured on a national morning TV show. Now a similar item is a big TV product hit. I wonder if somebody saw Joe working it first."

There are a bunch of videos on YouTube showing Joe at work. There are many other demonstrators, shown at work, too. Get mining on the online video sites and you will find lots of ideas. Make a list of words you want to use in the search field – get started and you will get better as you go along. The important thing is that you can do this without leaving home and it is a no expense way to look for star products, bonuses, demonstrations and ideas.

Business and Product TV Shows

This is where the world of the entrepreneur and the electronic age come together. Their meeting can be of tremendous value to product finders. They may be inventor shows set up as competitions - like an "American Idol" for new ideas. Or they may be a show where people with new ideas get to present them to would be investors. What are you looking for? Maybe not so much the products that win an investment - because you will probably be too late to get on board with those. But there can be good items that the investors take a pass on. Sometimes they can be right to pass and you need to be bright enough to figure out if this is the case. Other times maybe they are just a little too conservative in their thinking - or perhaps they are not looking for that category of items that is suitable for TV marketing. As clever as the panelists on these shows are they can also miss what you see as an obvious benefit - by "thinking outside the box" you may discover a different approach. You may think of how you can build a "product package" with some dynamic bonuses. If you've studied my writings carefully you will remember to think of the potential for a demonstration. Not long ago I was at a major home show and I actually saw a product that had won an investment on one of these TV shows. The inventor was using part of the investment funds to exhibit at this show. So far so good - however, an important point was missed. The item was obviously a product that could be demonstrated, with both visual and verbal appeal. But these guys were just telling folks about it one on one and in quite a laid back way. I can only think they thought this was a away to "get the word out" as opposed to proving the product by selling a few thousand units. Neither the inventor nor the investor had picked up on this way to promote the product in the very home show that was famous for this approach. Here are a few of these TV shows to look out for:

Dragons' Den - a terrific show that runs on BBC America. You can also find it (and other shows mentioned here) online. Here's a link: http://www.bbcamerica.com/content/323/index.jsp

Or just go to Google and type in the name of a show to find more – including discussion boards.

Shark Tank – it's the USA program in the style of Dragons' Den and promises to be great as it develops. Kevin Harrington, one of the most successful "As Seen On TV" product promoters in recent times, is one of the panelist investors.

Here's a link:

http://abc.go.com/primetime/sharktank/index?pn=index

The Apprentice – this gets a lot of exposure.

The Apprentice UK – This can also be seen on BBC America when they repeat it

(These last two are not the format that seeks investors but some segments are related to products. And looking at what Alan Sugar, of The Apprentice UK, achieved with products – well that was a motivating adventure all on it's own.)

Pitchmen - the iconic show with the late Billy Mays - Pitchman Supreme - and Anthony "Sully" Sullivan. You'll see many products on these shows. But, once again, look for those that they take a pass on - mind you, these guys don't miss much but you never know your luck. What you will learn is what to look for in a TV product and what to look for in a demonstration. Plus, it's a great way to hone your skills. Remember, when viewing these shows, to always look for winners that the experts may have missed. **If you don't see the shows on TV look for them on the Internet.**

This seems like a good place to pay tribute to Billy Mays who passed on at the tender age of 50 years. Billy packed a lot into those 50 years and he is missed by many. Having started his career demonstrating products on the Boardwalk of Atlantic City he went on to be the most recognized TV Pitchman ever. More than that, here was a man who used his talents to help those in need of a helping hand. People who had a product and needed to sell it in order to seriously change their lives - well Billy helped them develop the product, get it manufactured, get finance for it and find a promoter to sell it on TV. Billy had to believe in a product to sell it and that can be a lesson for us all. He inspired and motivated more people than we will ever know - it could be in the millions. Billy Mays never lost touch with regular people. Hopefully his legend and motivation can continue in the airing of his TV spots and programs. I encourage you to watch his TV spots and shows and use them as an ongoing source of motivation and inspiration – it's a great way to hone your skills. This giant of a man definitely left us too early and will be missed. Thank you Billy.

Internet and Search Engines

In this day and age, the Internet is an amazing way to find products. Just prepare a plan before you start. You will need to have an idea of the category of item you are looking for, then make a list of keywords to work with. There will be some trial and error but you can work at it to get better. Use Google and other search engines to do you exploring. It is exploring, because one "road" will lead you to another and so on. Look for inventors, manufacturer, product catalogs and use your own thought process to lead you on. If you're getting nowhere then take a rest, think about it and try again. Companies in the Far East have literally thousands of product ideas – look for online directories that list them. Then go into the individual company websites – they are catalogs of products. Try this one to get you started: www.globalsources.com

Development Programs

It's no secret that governments and large corporations develop some amazing products, materials and techniques that never see the light of day outside of research departments. Many are developed for a purpose but don't prove to be successful. Now, many of these can be high tech, complex items outside the scope of what you will be looking for. However some byproducts, or "spinoffs" as they have come to be known, do find their way into the consumer marketplace. NASA development has been responsible for, among many other things, fire resistant materials, swimsuits that reduce drag, and, perhaps the most famous spinoff, so called "memory foam" which is used for a whole bunch of products. The best known of these is probably the mattresses we see advertised all the time. How about Velcro and microwave ovens? It's just a rumor that both of these came out of NASA development, as they were conceived at least a decade before NASA. Microwaves were an idea that sprang out of radar experiments at the Raytheon Corporation. While, the very useful, Velcro was a joint effort between a Swiss mountaineer and a French weaver.

Here are a few links to explore some more:

http://www.nasa.gov/home/index.html

Spinoff is a NASA publication that features successfully commercialized NASA development.
.
http://www.nasa.gov/home/hqnews/2006/feb/HQ_06055_Spinoff_2005.html

http://www.sti.nasa.gov/tto/

http://www.spacecoalition.com/products.cfm

The following is a fabulous archive of NASA "Spinoffs" – you'll enjoy digging around in here. Much of the stuff you'll skim by - but ideas may be prompted along the way.

http://www.sti.nasa.gov/tto/spinoff_spotlight_archive.html

Spinoff has a database of all technology that has been published since it started. If you think up a new idea for an existing development NASA are very open to approaches. Study the NASA website at the links above and it will take you in the right direction to make contact. Dig around on Google and you will find much more in the development area – where huge budgets have been spent and discoveries are waiting for other applications.

Time to think

Always give yourself time to think. Don't try to do all of the above at once and don't fragment your efforts. Focus is so very important in your goal to be successful. So, start off by focusing on one or two of the methods I've outlined above. Read the other sections that I have written and write up a short plan of what you intend to do – be sure to include something from each section. Don't just think of a plan – write it down… there can be huge difference in where this will take you. Think of a written plan like it being your road map – you'd never start a journey to a new city without a road map because, at best, you'd have trouble getting there. I think you get the picture! Look over your map often and use it to help you focus and refocus.

Resources

The Internet is a fabulous resource. But, don't forget that people are a resource too. I've written about inventors - but wait, there's more! The DRTV business, and the money that can be made from it, has generated a population of folks who are working on new ideas. Now,
these people are out there and you just need to find them or have them find you. Get the word out that you are looking for new items tor TV marketing - use press releases, classified ads in newspapers and online, set up a website and promote it. Online groups can be useful too, you can even use bulletin boards in local supermarkets and elsewhere. Try to get on local talk shows - radio and TV, plus write articles for publications. Offer to give talks to local groups, like the chamber of commerce, rotary clubs, condo residents, veterans clubs, senior citizen groups, business groups and more. The list goes on and you need only stop at the boundaries of your own

imagination (and there shouldn't be any). Always remember to carry your business card to hand out and advertise what you do.

How about social networking and online advertising sites? Use Linkedin, Twitter, Facebook, eBay, Craig'sList and others to look for products and promote the fact that you are looking for new products suitable for TV marketing. Use the value of live networking, online networking and any kind of networking to interact and find new ideas.

Here (below) are a few websites you can try in order to find venues to locate products. Do your research first. Don't just go there - use the Internet, or make phone calls, to see if the event will be worth your visit. This is a list of sources for shows, fairs and other events. Obviously these sites may change, move or be removed from time to time. But they will also give you an idea what to look for when you are using search engines to find events and places to prospect. Also, check with your local convention center and fairgrounds for various shows and events. By the way, any big hardware or housewares trade shows are worth checking out.

Also note this, if you can't get to a particular show you may be able to get a show directory with product listings. Just call up the show promoters, tell them you missed the show, and ask for the directory. Many times they will oblige. Or, sometimes the company and product listings are online.

If you have a product, be sure to check "The Easy Way to Finance" for introductions to companies in the industry who are constantly looking for TV Items.

Manufacturing Resources:

If you have a product (or an idea for one) and need to find a manufacturer or supplier, an interesting site is www.alibaba.com - it's a huge online directory, check it out.

Another useful website is: www.globalsources.com an online directory with sources for a great volume of products.

Be sure to look for manufacturers in the USA too. If they need the business they should give good pricing and there are cost savings on shipping and a long overseas pipeline between manufacturing and delivery. Some manufacturers can arrange to fulfill the products (shipping directly to customers) right from the factory. These days you can easily locate manufacturers on the Internet or through various trade associations

But when you deal with manufacturers or suppliers you need to be careful in protecting your ideas and products. Get some advice, if you are new to this area, maybe from a lawyer you know well or a family member who is in business – somebody you can trust. Never be shy about asking for help. Always remember to negotiate the best deal for the product cost. It is not a matter of being fair (although this is important) but of being realistic. You need to be able to allow a product promoter a 5 to 1 markup and it all starts with the raw cost of the product – then you need to consider shipping and other expenses you have to pay the manufacturer. It's not as simple as taking a cost price and multiplying by 5. Rather, you need to start with assessing what would be a realistic retail price for the item. How much will it sell for and does this price represent great perceived value? Based on this you can figure out how much to pay for the product in order to get the desired markup.

Design Sources

You may find a product that is ready made with manufacturing set up. However, sometimes you may want to create an item based on an idea or take an existing item and develop it to perform better or look more appealing. When you have a product or idea and want to take it to the design or prototype stage you can find designers on the internet – look around and choose carefully.

Here is a link to one such company:

http://www.designmyidea.com/started-new1.php

Graphic Designs

For graphic designs such as packaging, sales sheets or brochures – any graphics that can be printed – check out:

http://www.99designs.com/

They will have multiple designers create designs for your perusal and you choose what meets with your approval.

Check the lists following....

See the following resources....

Check This List:

Look through this list, and use it, but remember that you can find many shows and events by using search engine sites on the Internet.

State Fairs and County Fairs

http://www.ncstatefair.com/

http://www.weekendevent.com/statefairs.htm

http://honeymoons.about.com/cs/activeadventures/a/statefair_2.htm

http://dir.yahoo.com/Entertainment/Events/Fairs_and_Parties/State_Fairs/

http://dir.yahoo.com/entertainment/events/fairs_and_parties/county_fairs/

http://www.festivals-and-shows.com/state-fairs.html

Home Shows

http://www.homeownernet.com/events.html

http://www.homeshows.com/

http://www.homeshows.net/

http://www.southernshows.com/

http://www.freehomeshow.com/?gclid=CIXCq4fjrZoCFQJ2xgodqHpocA

http://www.acshomeshow.com/

http://www.showtechnology.com/?gclid=CKvv5bjjrZoCFQNbxwodRD-zcg

http://www.homeshownet.com/

http://www.osbornejenks.com/

http://www.showevent.com/

http://www.exposwest.com/

Trade Shows

http://www.nationalhardwareshow.com/app/homepage.cfm?appname=100562&moduleID=4731&LinkID=31470

http://www.buildingonline.com/news/viewnews.pl?id=4831

http://www.housewares.org/show/info/

http://expo-world.net/events/gourhouse.php

http://www.newageretailer.com/PageID/221/default.aspx
http://www.biztradeshows.com/

http://www.biztradeshows.com/usa/

http://www.tradeshowweek.com/

http://www.entrepreneur.com/marketing/marketingbasics/tradeshows/article44420.html

http://tradeshowcalendar.globalsources.com/TRADE-SHOW/Country/US/United-States.HTM

http://www.tradeshowsusa.com/en/Exhibition/usa/?region=195&country=228

http://tradeshow.tradekey.com/list/country/223/USA.htm

http://www.bvents.com/

http://www.bvents.com/co-usa/

http://www.americasgiftshow.com/

http://www.tradeshowhandbook.com/directory.html

Invention Shows

http://inventors.about.com/gi/dynamic/offsite.htm?zi=1/XJ/Ya&sdn=inventors&zu
=http%3A%2F%2Fwww.inventionconvention.com

http://www.inpex.com/

http://www.inventhelp.com/international-invention-trade-shows.asp
http://www.loveinventions.com/invention-shows-2008

http://www.britishinventionshow.com/show/index.html

Craft Shows

http://www.craftsfaironline.com/Listings.html

http://www.tsnn.com/

http://artfairsourcebook.com/

http://www.craftsfairguide.com/

http://www.craftsitedirectory.com/craftshows/index.html

http://www.craftcanada.com/

http://www.huffspromo.com/

http://www.artandcrafts.com/

http://www.wheretheshowsare.net/

http://www.wheretheshowsare.com/

Markets

http://www.keysfleamarket.com/

http://collectors.org/FM/

http://www.greatfleamarket.com/

http://www.webcrawler.com/webcrawler300/ws/results/Web/flea+market+guide/1/417/TopNavigation/Relevance/iq=true/zoom=off/_iceUrlFlag=7?_IceUrl=true&gclid=CL2qv9rqrZoCFQLixgodPCp_cQ

http://www.amazon.com/U-S-Flea-Market-Directory-3rd/dp/0312264054

http://fleamarket.about.com/od/findafleamarket/tp/PopularUSFleaMarketsHub.htm

http://fleamarket.directoryusa.biz/selectstate.php

http://www.nwfleamart.com/fmldirectory/index.php

Sewing - Crafting - Quilting - Scrapbooking Shows

http://www.rustybarn.com/2009-shows.html

http://www.blogcatalog.com/topic/home+sewing+show/

http://www.sewing.org/scripts/blog/2009/03/

http://www.getcreativeshow.com/

http://www.getcreativeshow.com/sewing_show.htm

http://www.csnf.com/

http://sewing.patternreview.com/cgibin/review/readreview.pl?ID=1620

http://www.findstitch.com/directory/by_category.cgi/cid,34

http://www.dmoz.org/Arts/Crafts/Events/

http://dir.yahoo.com/Business_and_Economy/Shopping_and_Services/Arts_and_Crafts/Crafts/Craft_Fairs/?o=a

http://www.sewing-stash.com/pages/Events_and_Groups/

http://www.world-design-directory.com/events/fabric.wdd

http://www.partyguideonline.com/recreation/crafts.html

http://dotcom.dir.mobi/index.php?c=Arts/Crafts/Events
http://www.google.com/Top/Arts/Crafts/Events/

http://www.google.com/Top/Regional/Europe/United_Kingdom/Recreation_and_Sports/Hobbies/Crafts/Events/

Scrapbooking Events

http://www.dmoz.org/Arts/Crafts/Scrapbooking/Events/

http://www.google.com/Top/Arts/Crafts/Scrapbooking/Events/

http://au.dir.yahoo.com/Arts/Crafts/Scrapbooking/

http://www.memoriesscrapbookingexpo.com/ohforexhibitors.asp

http://www.scrapbookexpo.com/

http://www.scrapbookusaexpo.com/

http://www.scrapbookingsuppliesonline.com/scrapbook_expo.asp

http://www.eventbrite.com/org/45764122

Quilting Events

http://www.dmoz.org/Arts/Crafts/Quilting/Events/

Food Shows and Events

http://www.partyguideonline.com/foodndrink/food.html

http://www.foodreference.com/html/upcomingfoodevents.html

http://www.agmrc.org/media/cms/foodtradeshows109_FB13E7CC2647E.pdf

Canada - Various Shows

http://www.toronto.worldweb.com/Events/FairsExhibitions/

Ireland

http://showcaseireland.com/

UK

http://www.idealhomeshow.co.uk/

http://www.springfair.com/page.cfm/action=Archive/ContentID=1/EntryID=1897

Festivals

http://www.craftlister.com/

http://www.fairsfestival.com/

http://www.ask.com/web?q=festival+list&o=14219&ifr=1&qsrc=999&l=dis

http://www.festivals.com/

http://festivalsandevents.com/

http://www.southfest.com/

http://festivalnet.com/

Also note that you can find most shows under categories that appeal to you by using Google and other search engines.

Remember to check shows out online before making a trip. It's easy to figure out if an event suits the category of product you are looking for. Checking will also let you know if dates or venues have changed.

If you have a product, be sure to check "The Easy Way to Finance" for introductions to companies in the industry who are constantly looking for TV Items.

Categories

You will see this later but it is here in the context of your search for items to be sold on TV. You will see many categories but I want to narrow your focus to those that have shown repeated success over many years.

Categories of Direct Response TV Products

Housewares & Home Appliances
Kitchen and Cooking Products
Hardware
Tools
DIY
Craft Items
Automobile Items
Demonstration Items
Cleaners
Sleeping Helpers (including mattresses and toppers)
Fitness and Slimming Products
Beauty and Look Good Categories
Weight Loss
Skin Care & Beauty
Pain Relief
Vitamins and Supplements
Motivational & Self Improvement Tapes, Discs and Books
Business Opportunities
Hobby Products
Musical Compilations
Collectibles
Heritage and Ancestry

Volume 2

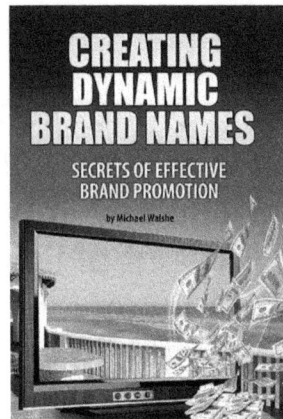

Creating Dynamic Brand Names

Secrets of effective brand promotion

How to create dynamic brand names

The Blatant Approach

I have a simple system for creating brand names for products and I urge you to follow it, as the brand name will, most times, serve to project the image of your product. This is particularly important in TV direct response selling as there is only a limited amount of time to get the sales message across to the viewers and if the name you choose automatically tells them what the item is designed to do or achieve you will be on the road to making your point. Think of some of the names you see on TV today, and in the past, and bear in mind that many of the currently successful TV product promoters are sticking to the same guidelines that were employed by their predecessors back in the early days of TV advertising. If you remember only two words in this regard that word should be **"BLATANCY"** and **"DESCRIPTIVE"** Be **BLATANT** and **DESCRIPTIVE** in all aspects of getting your message across and even the slowest viewer will understand. After all why leave this to chance? When I think of **BLATANCY** and **DESCRIPTIVE,** names like Miracle Painter, Chinese Wok and Veg-O-Matik instantly come to mind because they immediately conjure up an image of the product and what it does. A name like Magic Pens tells me in a flash that there is something special about this product, it gets my attention and tells me I should watch and find out more. Words like Miracle, Super, Power, Easy, Quick, Master coupled with a **DESCRIPTIVE** word like Knife, Slicer, Painter, Saw, Tool, or Cookware tell me that; a) there is something special about the item and; b) exactly what the product is, no guessing is required. The phrase O-Matic or A-Matik projects the message that the item I am being presented with will automatically do what it is supposed to do, or perhaps just as automatically solve a problem. I feel sure that by now you will have got my point and that, my friends, just about sums up what I mean by **"BLATANCY"** and **"DESCRIPTIVE"**.

Brand Name that says; "This is the only one"

On the other hand sometimes I may want to create a sense of mystique in the prospective customer's mind and this can be achieved by creating a brand name which links a sales concept to the product and essentially is interwoven with the particular item and what it does. A prime example of this approach can be seen in the Ginsu Knife brand name which was originally used in conjunction with a karate chop, of a tomato, as an opening scene to the TV commercial, this was quickly followed by the appearance of a Japanese chef who was about to use the knife.   Close up shots of the knife and other items in the set went on to visually demonstrate this product's outstanding sharpness and other desirable attributes. In short time an aura of Japanese sharpness, sturdiness and quality was established. This banner also helped to keep "copy cat" versions away from the market place because would be competitors had not only the need to "knock off" a knife they also were faced with the task of recreating the Ginsu image, mystique and the credibility implied by the way this item had been presented. This placed competitor's products in the position of automatically being cast in the role of "me too" copies, while the buying public wanted, and had been sold on, the original.

My System for Choosing a Brand Name

The approach I take really is simple so if you have previously thought there was something complex or mysterious or about creating a brand name believe me when I say that you were off base. Using the criteria outlined above as my guidelines, I simply write down every name that comes to mind that would be appropriate for the product. I leave no ideas out and do not decide on keeping or dismissing any potential name, which comes to mind, at this stage. In other words, I allow my mind to think freely with no constraints or boundaries. Then, when I have the most exhaustive list, which I can come up with, I set out to gradually whittle it down. I do this by using a process of elimination. First I delete the weakest names and continue doing this through several passes until I have a short list. If this list is hard to choose from, I have achieved my objective up to this point and continue to pare it down until I am satisfied that my number one choice will blatantly tell a would be buyer a) what the item is and; b) that it is special in some way and therefore worthy of a closer look. If I decide to take the route of creating a mystique or an image for the product, which will marry to a sales concept that I have in mind, I must be careful to effectively make this link in a TV viewer's mind without he or she having to think hard about it. In other words it must be immediately obvious. I use basically the same system for selecting domain names and you will read more on this below.

Protecting Your Brand Name

Protection of your chosen name is very important to you and for this reason when I address this issue, or any other matter involving legalities, You should take the advice of a competent attorney. Do make sure this attorney specializes in trademark work. This doesn't need to cost a fortune and should be approached in the same way as you would shop for any other supplies or services. Shop around, talk to a few lawyers and get comparative pricing. Do not be embarrassed to negotiate just like you would for any other commodity or service and always, when you are starting out, or later in business, seek out the best price bearing in mind that you also require reliability and competence in this area. If you are just starting out in business let the lawyer know this and make it clear that you are on a tight budget at this time but it is your plan to be successful in the business and this will mean more work for your attorney and other services that you will be using. Lawyers need business just like the rest of us and the realistic ones know that they have to sow seeds now in order to reap rewards later. In order to save money please don't be frightened to use expressions like "that's more than I expected to pay at this time" or "I'm afraid I don't have that much in my budget.... could you do it for less?" When you ask a question like this or when you seek any concession you must at that point stop talking in order to give the person on the other side of the table a chance to respond, if you keep talking this will deprive him or her of the opportunity to answer. Sometimes there may be an awkward pause but when you have posed the question simply look the person in the eye and wait.   As in any game, and that's how you should look on certain aspects of business, the object is to win.... win points.... win rounds.... win games.... win battles..... win discounts. But do strive to always win. Anyway, back to the subject of protecting your brand name, with the proviso to have the approach you take confirmed as correct by a lawyer's advice and opinion. I always proceed on the basis that using the marking TM (standing for Trade Mark) will afford me proof, if ever I am required to do so, of the date on which I first publically used the name in what is known in inter state commerce. In this way I can prove this use was prior to the name being used by anyone else. Broadly speaking this can be achieved by selling a quantity of the product to a customer in a state other than the one I am based in. I must then ship this consignment across a state line. The brand name should be affixed to the items by means of a label, marked in some way directly on the products, also print it on the product's packaging. Please be sure to check all this with a lawyer, as laws and regulations can change – and, in any case a lawyer should have more precise knowledge. Please bear in mind that I am only referring to the USA, as the laws of other countries may be different in some respects and you must therefore seek proper legal advice. Having established the use of the name, or even before this, you can take steps to have it registered and once again I would urge you to use a lawyer's services, particularly in the early stages of your career in this business. As a first step to registering, the attorney will do a search to determine whether the proposed Trade Mark is being used by anyone else, either on a federal (nationwide) basis or in a particular state. You may choose to do this legwork yourself, particularly if you wish to initially use the Trade Mark on an unregistered basis in order to test the viability of the product. A lot of the research can be done on the Internet.

Go to: http://www.uspto.gov/

This is where you can find much information on how to go about searching.

This is a US Government website devoted to Intellectual Properties such as Patents, Trademarks and Copyrights. Certainly ensure that a search is undertaken prior to committing to any major expenditure such as the creation of packaging or any form of advertising and prior to using a brand name in other ways. There are also certain directories that can be used for this purpose, some are on CD Rom for ease of use, and you may be fortunate enough to find them in your local library. A search on the Internet should help find some directories too. Do, however, make sure that any publication of this nature is the current issue as most are updated periodically. It is for this reason that I don't list any – by using the Internet, or enquiring at your local library, you can find current publications. Of course, one benefit of using a lawyer for the search is that many have access to on line databases that are kept current. Here are some websites that show patents:

http://www.freepatentsonline.com/5329728.html

http://www.patentstorm.us/patents/5586413/description.html

http://www.wipo.int/pctdb/en/wo.jsp?wo=2004093612

But, like I say above, whatever you find out be sure to check it with your lawyer.

Domain Names

The same approach to creating a brand name should be used when selecting and registering a domain name. Many of the orders derived from a TV advertising campaign will be taken on the web. Having a strong domain name that is linked to your brand name is extremely important and will strengthen your position. Remember these two words in this regard - **"BLATANCY"** and **"DESCRIPTIVE**" keep them in mind. Be **BLATANT** and **DESCRIPTIVE** in choosing a domain name and it must "mirror" your brand name. In this way you will be projecting your message right the way through all aspects of promotion and advertising. Also, make sure you keep renewing the registration in plenty of time.

There is power in having a strong domain name related to your product. The reason being that now a big portion of TV product sales are made from a website. Whereas, at one time most orders were taken by using a toll free phone number or by mail.

Here is a suggested approach to registering a domain name for your product. You may also have good ideas as you start to think about this subject. The choice is in order from the top down:

Product name – (example only) Miracle Cookware

Domain name 1 – MiracleCookware.com
Domain name 2 – MiracleCookwareOffer.com
Domain name 3 – BuyMiracleCookware.com
Domain name 4 – OrderMiracleCookware.com
Domain name 5 – GetMiracleCookware.com

There can be other variations and you can see that I always get the product name in the domain name. You may want to get all these variations registered. This will give you more control and also help you against would be competitors. As many names are already registered, you may even want to pick a name for your product that you are sure you can get registered. Just pick the name, check if it's available as a trademark, and do the registration for the domain right then. Registration and renewal is not expensive these days. Having a domain name to include in the deal can help in your discussions with a TV products promoter. A memorable domain name is also useful for paid search word advertising. Would be TV buyers will remember the name and can put it in the search engine to find your product – maybe days or weeks after seeing the TV spot.

In Summary

I have deliberately kept this issue simple, short and to the point. At the risk of being repetitive, however, let me seek to drive my message home. A good and strong brand name – and domain name - is extremely important in the TV Direct Response business or in any selling arena where you are relying on a certain amount of impulse to influence the buying decision. The reason being that in this day and age most people are very busy, plus they are constantly being bombarded by an enormous amount of information on a wide variety of subject matter. Therefore most of us automatically allocate a certain amount of our attention to a particular subject depending on our interest level. Some matters get no attention at all, but you may be sure that you will have your customer's attention only for a limited time and you must keep him or her interested. Think of this allocation of attention time as the amount of time that your sales message is allowed to stay in a person's mind, get boring even for an instant and you will face instant eviction. There is an expression that says you need to "cut through the clutter". So please... please keep it SIMPLE and don't send your message over people's heads or make it so it's beyond their instant understanding. The brand name Shur-Lok Wrench immediately tells me that here is a wrench that will lock on tight and hold on until it's loosened a nut and that, folks, is a SIMPLE message.

Some brand names and the messages they were designed to project. These examples make the point I have laid out above.

Miracle Painter – What can be stronger than a Miracle? Coupled with the descriptive word "Painter" this tells what the product does. A strong name and easy to grasp right away.

Armourcote Cookware – Pans were all over store shelves. We set out to promote the surface of this new cookware set.

Ginsu Knife – Japanese chefs were known to wield sharp kitchen knives so what could make the point of super sharpness better. Coupled with the mystique of the Orient, this set the Ginsu out on its own and copies were just not the original. This is one of the most remembered brand names in the history of DRTV and it was coupled with a TV spot opening that many have never forgotten all these years later. The karate chop on a tomato certainly got the attention of viewers.

Miracle Slicer – Another with the Miracle theme. Not just any slicer but the Miracle Slicer. This labeled the outstanding and the descriptive word let you know straight away what this product was all about. Oh – the fast paced visual demos helped too!

Chinese Wok – Simple and descriptive yet powerful. The name says exactly what the item is and, being a Chinese Wok, you know it is original. This name projects strong credibility – a little mystique, yet you know what it is instantly.

Shur-Lok Wrench – What do you want from a wrench? You need it to lock on tight and not slip. Plus, you need strength. This name says it all.

Rocket Chef – A manual food processor and so easy to use – this name says it all. Rocket = Speed and Chef = Gourmet Food Preparation.

Titanium II Knives – Titanium suggests both strength and hi-tech. A knife set for the modern world.

Further Summary – Just To Make It Clear

Even though you at selling a product always remember that it is being sold on TV by the effective use of words and pictures. So, in choosing a brand name always remember that you are essentially selling its word or words.

Picture in your mind how the brand name will look on TV screens. Will it be instantly memorable? This means it needs to be uncomplicated and not seeking to project some obscure image. I always like to say a brand name for TV must be blatant.

Then mentally project a step forward to visualize how it will look on packaging placed on store shelves. Will it have a presence that people are strongly aware of as the item they saw in TV advertising? Is it blatant in how it describes the product? Is it simple yet still powerful? In short, you should not have any complication as to what product this brand name relates to.

Go to any website that sells As Seen On TV items and browse thought the product names to see how they fit what I am saying here.

Now that domain names also serve as an effective banner for a brand it is important to choose a domain name that matches the brand name. But can you register the domain name you want? It is best to lock both names down at the same time and many times your selection will be governed by domain name availability.

If you are presenting your product to one of the companies that promote on TV it will be a strong help to have an effective brand name together with a domain name that complements it. A product that has the elements required to make it suitable for selling on TV, together with a dynamic brand name and a domain name that matches it, is a powerful package to present.

Volume 3

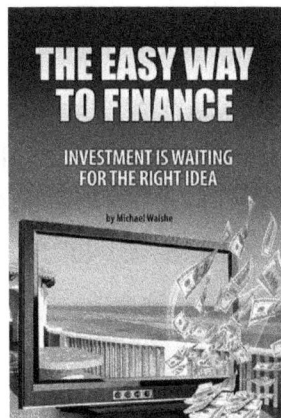

The Easy Way to Finance

Investment is waiting for the right idea

How To Get Finance For Your Project

The easy way is to use the financial resources of a company that is in the business of promoting and selling TV products. These promoters (you will see me refer to them as promoters in many places) need products and you may have a winner for them – you need them to sell your product and finance TV production and promotion. In some deals they may finance manufacturing and product inventory. The object is to create a "win – win" relationship that benefits both parties.

The major point is that these companies need a continuous flow of new products in order to meet the expenses of running their business and making profit. In this situation there are key promoters who will be receptive to new products that meet the criteria for a winner that I lay out in these pages.

The Easy Way to Finance

Getting finance for an idea that has winning potential can be the easiest thing in the world if you know how to go about it.   The reason for this is that in the TV Direct Response and mail order world there are many companies, as I have said, let's call them promoters, just waiting for, and actively seeking, new ideas and new products. They need them to make their businesses succeed and in many instances they are desperate for products to keep their businesses going.   In this context you, the ideas person, are in the driving seat. So I'm not going to tell you to go to your local bank or to seek finance from conventional sources.   If, for instance, a TV Direct Response company likes the idea or product which you present to them, and if they feel they can make money from it, they will be delighted to put up some finance in order to move the project forward. But don't be over eager just because there is money on the table, your idea may be worth hundreds of thousands or even a million or more dollars.   At this stage protection is the key word to remember.   If your idea is patented you will feel that you are in good shape but please remember that patents are not invincible, they can often be got round. For this reason your proposal to a promoter must contain a provision for protection, this is usually known as a non-disclosure agreement. Once again, you must get this from an attorney because interpretation of any legal document is subject to change and you must use what is right for you at the given time.

A Proposal With Protection

Your approach to a promoter will be to have this company market and sell your products and this will be coupled with finance. So you must choose a company with a strong track record of sales and not just go with one that will put up the money. As TV Product sales are blatantly in public view finding such promoters is not too difficult. You initial approach should be succinct and easy to follow. It is always important to remember that executives of major corporations are being constantly bombarded with all kinds of information. Your approach will get attention if you cut through the clutter by keeping your information short, sweet and to the point. Fortunately for you most people have no idea how to do this and some even ramble on to the point of being impossible to understand. Do not make your first approach with a multi page presentation, no matter how interesting it may seem, as you will be in danger of losing the readers attention. Worse still, you may be consigned to the pending tray to be lost forever.   One page outlining your offer is all that is required as a first attention getter. You should give facts that interest the reader while protecting your secret information. This may sound difficult but as you read on you'll find it's actually very simple.

See the following for example of a letter to a promoter....
To put you in the picture as to what I mean here's an example of a letter to a promoter:

John Smith
USA Media Corporation
100 American Plaza
Tinsel Town
Los Angeles, CA 00000

Dear Mr. Smith,

I have been referred to you by Michael Walshe who advises me that your company may have an interest in a new product that I have developed.

I am sure you will understand the need for a certain amount of confidentiality at this stage but I will mention that my item is related to the area of exercise and has been tested by several doctors and also sports trainers who speak highly of its capabilities, particularly in the area of effective thigh reduction.   It is possible that some of these experts may be inclined to give on camera testimonials provided they could be assured with regard to the credibility of the company handling the item's promotion. For this reason, even though there are other prospective interested parties, my first approach is to you.

If you are interested in receiving further information please contact me at your earliest convenience. In the meantime if you have any questions please feel free to call me at the above telephone number.

Very truly yours,

Thomas Jones

At this point you will not make any mention of the deal you are looking for, wait till you have the non-disclosure agreement in hand before going forward. You will ask for the signing of this at the next stage after you get positive interest. This will be the way you are seeking to protect the confidentiality, and look for only authorized use, of your idea.

Maybe a Telephone Call to Start the Ball Rolling

You may prefer to make contact on the phone but do your preparation first. Your goal should be to get an appointment for a meeting to discuss your product. So here are a few tips:

1. Be prepared for what you are going to say and have clear notes in front of you.

2. Make sure you have a good contact number that is going to lead you to the right person. You can usually find what you want – name and phone number – on the Internet.

3. I like to start at the top by asking for the President or CEO. He/she may not go very far with you but when he/she refers you to the right person in the company it's easier to get a hearing when you say (for example) - "Mr. Smith suggested I call you" – I think you get the point. If you are referred by the boss people tend to pay attention and give you the courtesy of a good hearing. When trying to get through to the top person be sure to mention that you have a product or idea that you believe can make his/her company a substantial amount of money. That usually gets attention these days.

4. If you get through to voice mail have your message in front of you (written down previously) and deliver it in a succinct, confident manner. Your message should be something like: "My name is Tom Murphy and I have a product to offer your company. I believe it can be a huge success on TV. I would like to discuss this further if you can call me on (leave your phone number) – thank you. Also mention "I believe my product (idea) can make a huge amount of money for your company" that should help. Never ramble on – no long messages.

5. When you talk on the phone remember your goal is to get an appointment not to tell what the product is at this stage. Most people understand the need for initial confidentiality but they do want to hear something before they agree to meet you and give you valuable time.

See what I have said in my example letter (above) and use a similar approach.

"I am sure you will understand the need for a certain amount of confidentiality at this stage but my item is related to the area of exercise and has been tested by several doctors and sports trainers who speak highly of its capabilities, particularly in the area of effective thigh reduction. It is also possible that some of these experts may be inclined to give on camera testimonials provided they can be assured with regard to the credibility of the company handling the item's promotion."

With a little thought you can write up something along these lines in regard to any product – and without disclosing what the item actually is. Include the general category of merchandise it comes under. Do it, write it up, and have it in your notes for your conversation on the phone.

The Next Stage

This will be to ask for signing of a non-disclosure agreement. If the company does not sign the agreement, or a revised form of it that is satisfactory to you and your attorney, you will move on and make your offer to the next prospect on your list. However, if you get a positive response, together with the non-disclosure agreement, you can move to the next stage. This will be to advise the company with an outline of the product, together with a sample or prototype, and at the same time tell them of the deal you are looking for. The approach to your product outline is covered elsewhere (see Product Outline at the end of this section). Include points from the section: A Successful TV Direct Response Product. But now let's address the deal. In the industry you will be dealing in there is no hard and fast set deal – there are guidelines. There is, however, a governing factor, very simply the deal must be attractive to the promoter and must be such that the cost of the product allows for a sufficient margin of profit after the other promotion and selling expenses. A rule of thumb is that TV Direct Response products should have a 5 times mark up.

Product Price or Royalty Option:

Please be aware that this will vary. Each deal tends to have it's own variables so, I will give here what I think is fair to both sides – you and the promoter. The goal is to help the product sell.

Will you own the product – either because you manufacture it or will purchase it, for resale, from the manufacturer? Will you, therefore, be in the position of selling the product to the promoter as, and when, this company requires it? If so, then you should include your profit in the price you quote to the promoter. This profit needs to be on all sales - and every potential form of income - in all markets and categories of sales.   Remember that the price you quote should allow for a 5 to 1 markup – if it sells, to the end consumer, at 20.00 then the cost price should be 4.00 including your profit. Now obviously you have to make a reasonable profit so if this forces you above the 20% cost there may be some leeway. But be prepared to explain why – you will be asked.

Now, let's say you don't own the product but have an exclusive sales agreement with the manufacturer – and do make sure you have this agreement in writing before going forward. In this case you can propose a deal whereby the promoter orders from the manufacturer and pays directly. In this deal there should be provision for the promoter or the manufacturer to pay you a royalty on all sales and in all categories of sale. The product price and the royalty combined should still allow for the 5 to 1 markup – or a little more if the situation warrants it, as I have explained above.

Royalty percentages vary and will depend, to a large extent, on who you are dealing with and their own business policies. But a guide is from 2% to 5%. In my opinion only huge volume should warrant the lower. When you work on a royalty basis this is an amount you will receive over and above the cost of the product. As I have said, there is no set amount for the royalty calculation, other than the need to keep costs at a point where the product has enough gross profit to allow it to sell.

Remember your royalty (or profit if you go with that option) should be paid on all sales – sales on TV based on the retail price (excluding shipping & processing / shipping & handling charges / and taxes), sales based on a wholesale price to a retailer, sales based on wholesale prices to overseas clients and so on. You need to get paid on all sales - and every potential form of income - in all markets and categories of sales.

As mentioned, the royalty when added to the cost of the product should not total more than 20% (giving a 5 times mark up for a 20.00 item).

Example:

Proposed Retail selling price: 20.00
Royalty @ 5% = 1.00
Cost of product = 3.00
So 3.00 + 1.00 = 4.00 that is 20% of 20.00

To express this clearly in your proposal let's keep it simple and easy to follow:

Proposed Product retail selling price: 20.00
Cost of product = 3.00
Royalty is 5% = 1.00
Total = 4.00 which is 20% of 20.00

Or

Proposed Product retail selling price: 20.00
Cost of product = 4.00 (including your profit)
Total = 4.00 which is 20% of 20.00

In Summary, if you are manufacturing and supplying the product yourself you can just quote a wholesale price. In this example it would be 4.00 including your profit. Otherwise quote the manufacturers price and add your royalty to be paid separately.

If the promoter wants to get the product manufactured elsewhere, say overseas in order to reduce costs, you can agree. As long as you get a royalty based on a 20.00 retail price (or whatever price the product sells for) and as long as any manufacturer you have an agreement with also agrees. In which case this manufacturer will expect to be paid in some way. Say, by making a royalty equal to his usual profit – or a little less. A benefit to you is that the promoter will be financing the manufacturing of the product and carrying inventory.

Licensing Deal:

This is a deal where a promoter commits to organizing manufacturing, carrying product inventory, advertising and promotion of the product and will pay you a royalty based on all sales and forever. This kind of deal has earned huge income over the years. A variety of licensing models can be applied. You could negotiate an up front payment – you will want this to be a free and clear payment. The promoter may want it to be an advance against future royalties. The deal you can get will depend on how much the promoter wants your product. On top of this lump sum payment you want a percentage of each unit of the product sold as your royalty – based on all sales. How do you figure out the amount of this percentage? Remember what I've said about the cost of the product allowing for a 5 to 1 markup and calculate what it will cost to manufacture the item. How much is left to allow you to get to the markup level? That is probably the maximum allowable for your royalty. But the promoter has work to do in arranging and monitoring manufacturing, and a cost in carrying inventory, so it's unlikely you can get the maximum. You could if you have a lot to contribute – for instance, if you are the person who can effectively pitch the product on TV. In any event, I would try to get 5% to 6% but not settle for lower than 2% on all sales –

remember that means on all sales in all markets and categories of sales. Now, here's an important point; you will be in a much stronger negotiating position if you have a patent or some other protection. This will put you, and the promoter, in a stronger position against would be competitors or "knock off artists" as they are referred to. You could ask for as much as 7% in a situation like this. Not that you have to stop there - but be realistic in understanding that all parties have to make money. The promoter knows the strength of protection and it puts more value in your product. It could even take you outside the 5 to 1 markup rule if there are savings that can be made elsewhere – say, in manufacturing, packaging, fulfillment or shipping costs. Some promoters may suggest (or you may explore this) that you have a 50/50 split of profits. This could be lucrative but you need to be careful as to how the word "profit" will be defined and what expenses will be charged against it. This needs to be carefully defined in the contract you enter into and you will need your lawyer to draft the language so that you are covered strongly.

Be Realistic:

Do bear in mind the need to be realistic when negotiating – yes, you want to get a reasonable royalty percentage or profit - but do remember that we are talking about high volume business. Simply put, TV sales are either huge or not at all. A promoter will test the product by producing a TV commercial and booking TV airtime. Then if the test is successful to the point that it can be expanded profitably it can get to the large volume expected from a nationwide TV campaign. If the test fails, everything stops and the promoter should hand the rights to the product back to you. The contract you negotiate, and this should be done with the assistance of a competent attorney, should specify this. So, simply put, with a nationwide campaign this equals big volume – with a failed test this equals no sales. I'm not trying to paint a bleak picture, as you always want to stay positive, just pointing out that unlike other forms of selling there is not always a degree of sales level in between. Sometimes there is, but not always – some products may come close to break even in a test and warrant a "tweaking" of the TV spot or the website upsells. Why am I telling you all this? Just to keep you realistic, in that you may have to negotiate a lower royalty rate so bear in mind that your royalty can multiply based on this high volume business. As the old saying goes: "you take dollars to the bank and not points" – it's a good point to always remember.

By taking this approach you will be allowing the promoter to make sufficient gross profit from the item to motivate the company to allocate a higher volume of TV time or print space advertising to its promotion. This in turn will generate a higher volume of orders and create a virtual spiral whereby the more product that's sold the more the item is pushed. Consider that the various products in a promoter's current collection of items are listed in order from the most profitable on down. Obviously the more profitable an item is means the more advertising money that is going to be allocated to it. With the high flyers being given the most attention that simply serves to making them fly even higher. The end result is that your royalty (or profit) multiplied by high volume sales can mean substantial dollars in your bank account. This of course will give you the stability and security to search for and develop more bright ideas, repeat the cycle and build a lucrative and enjoyable business.

Upsells:

These are products that are sold in addition to the basic item, but don't confuse them with bonuses that are sold, on TV, as part of the package. Upsells are offered on the phone, when the customer calls to order, or on a website if the customer orders online. For the purposes of negotiation, there are basically two categories of upsells: a) Those you offer to the promoter (your upsells) and; b) Those which the promoter decides to obtain from other sources (promoter's upsells). Either way they are designed to produce profit for the campaign and, therefore, give it a better chance of success. There is no set method for royalty payment on upsells and it really depends on getting the best deal you can negotiate.

Here are some approaches:

1. Look to get your full royalty percentage on all upsells.

2. Look to get your full royalty percentage on your upsells and a reduced royalty percentage on the promoter's upsells.

3. Look to get your full royalty percentage on your upsells and no royalty percentage on the promoter's upsells.

4. Look to get a reduced royalty percentage on all upsells.

The basis for you earning from upsells is that it is your TV product that is driving all these sales. However, do bear in mind that it is the promoter's financial investment and TV commercial that is also playing a huge part in this venture. Do please take note that there are many campaigns that are not profitable without a successful upsell program. Use this to help your product succeed and be ready to propose some upsells that can be compatible with you product. Very often, the first upsell will be a second package (the same as offered in the TV commercial) but at a reduced price to the customer. In this way customers can buy additional packages for friends or relatives. Another successful upsell can be an "upgrade package" whereby the basic package is offered with some accessories or complementary items.

If you don't want to do the negotiating yourself there are professionals who can help. I have been in the Direct Response TV industry since 1976 and in the business of developing products for even longer. I've picked up some knowledge and skills along the way and can handle the negotiations and placement of your product. However, I must be fair in mentioning that I am very selective and must like your product, this means I must feel it can be successful. If so, providing this interests you, I will look at having myself, or one of my associates, take on the handling of your product. You can contact me at:

Michael@MichaelWalshe.com if you have a product.

Variables

The Direct Response TV business is full of variables and this is particularly so in the costing of a product. I have referred to the need for a 5 to 1 markup and even this can have some variables. This can help you in making a deal because the promoter does have some room in the budget for other items – and this is over and above the allowance (20% of retail price) for the cost of the product. If this money is not required for your project, because the said items don't come into play, you may be able to justify some of it being used for your profit or royalty. Here are few items to watch for – they are costs that the promoter may be faced with paying. On the other hand, he may not and that may leave more money in the budget for you.

1. Royalty for a company (or person) to produce (and usually write) a TV commercial. Could you provide a written TV script with the product?

2. Royalty for talent to appear in the TV commercial. This would be for a spokesperson or demonstrator. Could you present your product on TV?

3. Royalty for a product finder. This could be you anyway.

4. Expenses or packaging. Will you provide the product in a, ready to ship, mail order box? If so, this saves money that the promoter may have budgeted for.

5. Fulfillment costs. Can you or the manufacturer do this? It involves, packing, labeling and shipping the product (not including shipping charges). If you can do it for a lower price than a fulfillment company, more money comes into play.

6. Weight of product. Lightweight items mean lesser shipping charges, so the promoter may be under budget in this area.

All this is worth looking into when considering your proposal to the promoter and figuring out how much may be available for you.

Intellectual Property Rights & Domain Names

All matters relating to intellectual properties should be discussed with an attorney who specializes in this field of law. Intellectual properties include copyrights, trademarks, patents, patents pending, industrial design rights, and trade secrets – your lawyer can advise you of any others, legal matters change from time to time. In this regard you will need to be advised about holding onto these rights, or if the product manufacturer owns the rights this manufacturer will need to get the legal advice in connection with this matter. If the product was mine I would always hold the rights. If necessary, to do a deal with a product promoter or any company wishing to sell the product, a licensing agreement can be entered into. Your lawyer can help you with this and provide the licensing agreement. In this way you keep control of the intellectual property and the licensee gets to use it for an agreed purpose. This is particularly important if your deal calls for you to be paid a licensing fee or royalty. By the way, a word about lawyers. Some of them can be slow moving (often because they are trying to handle too much work) and DRTV is a fast moving business. You need to let your lawyer know this and that you don't want to miss a potentially lucrative deal by moving slowly. Even so, you are the one affected most and you need to stay on top of the schedule and push to move the lawyer along.

The same approach, as above, should apply to any domain name that you have registered in connection with the product. I would retain ownership of this domain name and enter into an agreement to allow the product promoter to use it in connection with sales of the product. It is very easy to point the domain name to a site carrying the product. Or you can change the server info related to the domain. This may be on the domain registrar's site or where it is hosted. As easy as this may be, it is another area where you need the help of a specialist – a website technical person. Just make sure that it is done in such a way that you keep control of the domain name. Also, make sure you keep renewing the registration in plenty of time.

There is some power in having a strong domain name related to your product. The reason being that now a big portion of TV product sales are made from a website. Whereas, at one time most orders were taken by using a toll free phone number or by mail.
Here is a suggested approach to registering a domain name for your product. You may also have good ideas as you start to think about this subject. The choice is in order from the top down:

Product name – (example only) Miracle Cookware

Domain name 1 – MiracleCookware.com
Domain name 2 – MiracleCookwareOffer.com
Domain name 3 – BuyMiracleCookware.com
Domain name 4 – OrderMiracleCookware.com
Domain name 5 – GetMiracleCookware.com

There can be other variations and you can see that I always get the product name in the domain name. You may want to get all these variations registered. This will give you more control and also help you against would be competitors. As many names are already registered, you may even want to pick a name for your product that you are sure you can get registered. Just pick the name, check if it's available as a trademark, and do the registration for the domain right then. Registration and renewal is not expensive these days. Having a domain name to include in the deal can help in your discussions with a TV products promoter. A memorable domain name is also useful for paid search word advertising. Would be TV buyers will remember the name and can put it in the search engine to find your product – maybe days or weeks after seeing the TV spot.

The Deal

Your deal will be based on the understanding that the promoter finances all development and promotion of your product or idea from that point forward. This may involve further development of the product that will perhaps include expanding it into a more rounded and appealing package to make it more attractive for television or mail order selling. It will also require the production of a TV commercial or mail order advertisement and the scheduling of media buying, telemarketing, order taking and processing together with product fulfillment. Production of TV commercials and other advertising may require contracting production personnel and on air talent and both of these may involve payment of ongoing royalties. All of this will be the responsibility of the promoter and your deal should stipulate this.

Finance With Risk and Understanding

So, as you can see, there will be substantial money to be spent on what is essentially a risk venture. That is why it would be quite unlikely for a bank to invest in this type of enterprise without asking for very solid collateral in the form of real estate or some other type of tangible assets. On the other hand the promoters I am referring to understand their business and know whether a product has the right profile to potentially succeed. Do not be under any illusion, they are very selective but once they decide to go with an item they will push hard and fast to make it work. Time, to them, is equally as valuable as cash and they will be anxious to get your product to the market before any other company in their highly competitive industry finds out about it.

Your Presentation and One Big Tip

Prepare for the presentation and have all the facts about the product ready. This should include figures, prices and potential profit, potential sales volume, size of the market and so on. Add anything else that you think will help get your point across. Put it all in a short and succinct written presentation – just a few pages in a simple binder will do – and be ready to present it verbally too. Don't forget to include the demonstration (in its best sequence with the main benefits first) or individual demo points – put the strongest at the top. Outline what your product does and the problem that it solves. Be careful, in selecting a product, that it solves a problem of sufficient degree that people will spend good money to buy it. They may not want to buy a solution to a small problem. Make sure it's a big problem and that by solving it customers will save money, trouble, time or energy – better still, all four and still more. If your product can paint a room in an hour this will appeal to many. If it's an easy way to take a lid off a paint can that's not a big problem so it may not be a seller. On the other hand, the lid remover can be an interesting bonus. So the problem has to be big enough to motivate people to do something about it and to spend money for the solution. Solving a problem may be the biggest element in the success of a TV product. So be sure to examine the degree of the problem – ask yourself "Would I spend x amount of money to get over this problem? Or, would I live with doing it the old way?" Being honest with yourself and having the ability to say "NO" can sometimes be a valuable asset.

Here's the big tip. Having done all your preparation, and with an appointment to meet, will you still be nervous? Probably, and the old timers (like me) will tell you that if you're not nervous you won't be at your best. It may sound like a contradiction but this applies to performers and pitchmen, entertainers and athletes, comedians and public speakers. They all have to perform in an atmosphere where good timing is essential. Ask anyone who goes on the stage, sells on QVC or HSN, or makes live presentations for a living in any business. Many will tell you that a little dose of nerves can be an advantage that gives your presentation an edge. The main thing is to prepare all the facts and figures – have them ready to a point that you know you can rely on them. Then, when you start talking the nerves should take care of themselves and all will be right. The big secret is in the preparation.

While Your Mind is on Money

While your mind is on money here's a way to make some fairly quickly. Think of it as a stepping-stone and a way to make some seed money that you can use to get into the TV product business – where the big money is. Perhaps it's way to make a living while you are working at finding and developing a TV product. In the meantime what's wrong with making a few hundred or even a $1,000 a week or more? Of course, this will depend on your own ability and how hard you go at it - but all work and business does. You're not afraid of trying hard are you? Anyway, if you take a look at the bonus volume – "Create Your Own Job" - which I have included, you will find all the details. It's about a ready-made business that others are making money at right now. The monetary investment is low and potential rewards are high. So, as long as you are prepared to invest your time, you can be on the first steps to your own fortune. I started in my own business, many years ago, with start up money of about $25 and I can honestly say that I've never looked back. Anyway this is something to think about but you may be in a position where you don't need help to get started – if so, that's OK.

However, if you are interested, see the bonus volume "Create Your Own Job" – also ask me (send me an e mail at michael@michaelwalshe.com) for a disc with demo features contained in it – and then give us a phone call or send an e mail. This is an ideal business for anyone who is bright and can hold a reasonable conversation. It can also get you out and about in the shows or shopping centers where you can be "in the swim of things" with lots of products all around you. Another thing, it's a great opportunity for pitchmen who know how to present a product – and some may be reading this. Maybe those who are at the stage where they want to slow down a little and get off the box onto a wider platform.

But, take note of what I said – "anyone who can hold a reasonable conversation" should take a look. By the way, you may want to do a favor for a friend or relative so, if the bonus volume is not for you, why not pass the info on to someone who may be looking for a job. Then they can create their own job.

But wait there's more!

Before you go to the bonus volume, read the rest of these pages and find out about all the useful resources that you'll see below. Then be sure to read the pages of my volume titled

"A Successful TV Product" which includes my "Million Dollar" Secret.

Development and Introductions

The following company (it's my business) can introduce you to TV product promoters. This firm can also help you develop your product, the demonstration, the TV spot script and your presentation to promoters:

Michael Walshe
Sales Magic, Inc
E Mail: Michael@MichaelWalshe.com

If your product has potential for selling on one of the TV shopping channels we can introduce you to a rep company with the expertise to take your product to a buyer. If you want to go this route send me an e mail to the address above.

By the way, many of you may be thinking in terms of products for sale on TV in the USA. However, the DRTV industry has been very well developed in European countries too. If you have the right product, we can introduce you to some of the big players on that side of the Atlantic. Your product may need some development to get it in shape for the presentation, so we'll work on that. In some European countries they have 24 hour shopping channels and you can imagine they need a lot of products to fill all that airtime. So, while the companies running these channels are both entrepreneurial and hungry for products, the items have to be right for their way of doing business. That's where good preparation comes in – sometimes you may only get one shot and it pays to get it right. There are also opportunities in Latin America and Asia among other areas – in fact DRTV is now a worldwide industry – and the same points apply.

Websites

This company specializes in building websites for the DRTV business.

Ken Osborn or Fausto Del Ponte
Liquid Focus
1335 Wood Ave, Bridgeport, CT 06604
Phone: 866-892-0259
Website: www.LiquidFocus.com

The websites this company creates can give you an understanding of how a range of upsells can be compiled to sell when an order is taken for a product. The profit from these upsell products can help the overall profitability of the offer – they are very important in today's DRTV world. If you prepare a range of upsells to go with your product you can be ready to present them, as a package deal, to TV products promoters. You may even want to have your product and upsells prepared, and ready, on a website in advance of doing a deal. Of course you can then pick a suitable domain name, register and control it.

See next for product promoters....

Companies in the industry – Promoters:

Some leaders in the industry.... A place to start with my introduction....

When you make contact mention you have an introduction from Michael Walshe.

USA:

Bill Barlow
Pitch World
E mail: Bill.Barlow@pitch.tv

Kevin Harrington
14044 Icot Blvd.
Clearwater, FL 33760
Phone: 727-288-2738

Tim Harrington
Harrington Multi Media Marketing LLC
14375 Myerlake Circle
Clearwater. FL 33760
Phone: 727-230-1036

Bill McAlister
Media Enterprises Inc.
2607 Interplex Drive,
Trevose, PA 19053
Phone: 800-471-6123

Cecilia Turner
American Telecast Products, LLC
1230 American Blvd.
West Chester, PA 19380
Phone: 610-430-7800

Mick Hastie
Homeland Housewares, LLC
11755 Wilshire Boulevard
Suite 1150
Los Angeles, CA 90025
Phone: 310-996-7200

Bill Guthy or Greg Renker
Guthy-Renker

41-550 Eclectic St., Suite 200
Palm Desert, CA 92260
Phone: 760-773-9022

Robert R. Schnabel Jr.
Fitness Quest, Inc.
1400 Raff Road SW
Canton, Ohio 44750
Phone: 330-478-0755

Canada:

Rob Woodrooffe

Interwood Direct

PO Box 218 Station K
Toronto, Ontario, Canada M4P 2G5
Phone: 416-250-1665 x 2221

Richard J. Stacey

Northern Response (International) Ltd.

18 Skagway Ave

Toronto, Ontario, Canada M1M 3V1

Phone: 416-261-6699

UK:

Bill Barlow
Pitch World
Sutherland House
70-78 West Hendon Broadway
London NW9 7BT
England
Bill.Barlow@pitch.tv

John Mills
JML
JML House
Regis Road
London, NW5 3EG
United Kingdom
Phone: +44 (0) 20 7691 3800
E Mail: john.mills@jmlgroup.co.uk

Latin America:

Daniel Gorinstein
Premiere Exclusives
Blvd. Manuel Avila Camacho No. 40-C
Col. El Parque Naucalpan
Edo. Mex. C.P. 53398
Mexico
Phone: (52+55) 5395-4847
E Mail: servadmindg@att.net.mx

Here are very useful contacts with knowledge that spans categories:

You may know John Parkin from the many infomercials where he is a dynamic presenter. John's knowledge from many years of experience can be of help in introductions and preparation for your own presentations.

John Parkin
Glenmoor Farm
High Street
Low Pittington
Durham DH6 1BE
United Kingdom
Phone: +44 (0) 77-10306308

Inventions Radio Program

This program, presented by John Cremeans and Akos Jankura, can put your invention in front of people looking for successful products. The program asks for protected inventions and you may submit your item for free. If you are ready to move with your invention this is a way to get great exposure.

John Cremeans
Akos Jankura
My Cool Inventions
John@MyCoolInventionsRadio.com
www.mycoolinventions.com
Tune in to the program at: 970WFLA – iHeartRadio.com

Do remember to build a good relationship with whoever you decide to deal with. If your product is not accepted be sure to return with new items as they come along – these folks are constantly on the lookout for new merchandise. You will hear many make statements like:

"Keep trying us with new ideas and something may hit the spot – we're not in the business of selling dozens or hundreds, but millions when we can"

See Product Outline next and use this for an effective proposal to promoters.

When you are ready to have me do an evaluation of your product or idea you should also complete this Product Outline and e mail it to:

michael@michaelwalshe.com

Product Outline

Date:

Product Name or Title:

(*Note: Please attach photo)

Product Owner or Creator:
Name:
Address:

Contact person:
Phone:
Fax:
E Mail

Product Information:

Product:

Item Number:

Product description:

(*Note: Complete description with any special points. State what the product is made from. If it is sold as a set (or kit) include all items in description.)

Warrantee or Guarantee information:

Country of Origin:

Upsell Products
(*Note: these can be actual products or ideas)**:**

Marketing Information:
(*Note: For main product)

Features:

Benefits:

Problem that can be solved:
(*Note: Describe a problem that this product can solve)

Any specific claims:

Demonstrations
(*Note: List all):

Does this product have mass appeal and why?

If not, which niche group will the product appeal to?

Material Information

Normal shipping time (if applicable)
Days:

Product packaging:
Contents:

Weight (product and packaging):

Dimensions (Packed): Outer:
                              Inner:

Cost price of product:
(*Note: this should include your profit or royalty)

Anticipated retail price point:

Track record of sales in any category of business:
(*Note: Include details of business category)

Patent or other legal protection:

Is this a new or unique product? If so, explain why:

Does product have retail sales potential? If so, explain why:

Does product get used and need replacing?

Does product have potential for a continuity program? If so, why?

Is there a well known spokesperson available – or potentially suitable? Who is this?

Are there testimonials available? Give details.

*Delete where it mentions "Note" (above) before printing and completing for a promoter. Leave these notes in when you send the Product Outline to me.

Volume 4

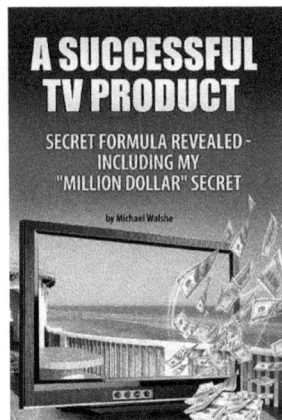

A Successful TV Product

Secret formula revealed –

Including my "Million Dollar" Secret

A Successful Direct Response TV Product

Profile:

These are necessary:

1. Demonstrations. Item must be capable of being demonstrated, visually and verbally.

2. Part of the demonstrations should show what I call a "magical transformation" or reveal a "valuable secret". It should contain what I call the "magic factor" – a dramatic part of the demo that really excites you and illustrates a benefit that makes the product so very special. The Ginsu Knife TV spot showed a can being cut through – this made the viewers say "wow". In my Family Name Origin & Meaning spot I reveal that the family name is a legacy given to unite your family. I'm sure you've seen TV spots where stains are removed before you eyes. You get the idea – all are examples of a "magical transformation" or a "secret revealed" – the "magic factor". This "magic factor" allows a producer to create what is called a "money shot" one that gets the phones ringing and brings in the money. If you are working on a demonstration for a product just ask yourself this; "If I had the ultimate power what would I make this product do?" Then see if the product can do it. That's how you find the most dramatic elements of a demonstration. Always put the strongest benefit as early as possible in

the demonstration. Then it should be used early in the TV spot in order to hold viewers attention and ensure they keep watching. If they're flipping channels a dramatic shot may stop them in their tracks. Express benefits in a dramatic way – be blatant – even over the top in putting the point across. But just as a means of expression and not, of course, in straying from the facts.

3. The product must solve a problem or provide an easy solution and the TV spot must get this point across strongly and early in the spot. Be careful on this point, a product must solve a problem of sufficient degree that people will spend good money to buy it. They may not want to buy a solution to a small problem. Make sure it's a big problem and that by solving it customers will save money, trouble, time or energy – better still, all four and still more. If your product can paint a room in an hour this will appeal to many. If it's an easy way to take a lid off a paint can that's not a big problem so it may not be a seller. On the other hand, the lid remover may be an interesting bonus item. So the problem has to be big enough to motivate people to do something about it and to spend money for the solution. Solving a problem may be the biggest element in the success of a TV product. So be sure to examine the degree of the problem – ask yourself "Would I spend x amount of money to get over this problem? Or, would I live with doing it the old way?"

4. Mass appeal. The masses use knives in their kitchen. Some niche appeal products can work too but they must be in a strong niche. Golf is a strong niche – butterfly collecting is not.

5. Product needs a 5 to 1 markup – divide the retail price point by the cost of the product – is the number 5? Profit is important. There are a lot of expenses involved in selling a product through Direct Response TV.

6. Strong perceived value at retail price point of the offer. Of course, the "magic price" point for selling on TV is $19.95 or less. Even as low as

$10 if the costs will allow it. But many items are sold successfully at higher prices – some at $100 or more. A $20 price point will reach out to a huge audience of receptive buyers but only if it is good value for money. On the other hand, a $100 item will have it's own pool of prospective buyers if it is good value for the item being offered.

7. A strong list of upsells – extra items that are sold when a customer calls to order. The upsells contribute, in varying degrees, to the profit of the campaign. They should be compatible with the basic product.

These are an advantage:

1. Proven success in some area of sales. Has your item sold in other areas of sales such as direct sales, retail or demonstration sales at shows and fairs? Proven sales success can put you a few steps up the ladder towards a winner.

2. A patent or other legal protection. Not essential but a distinct advantage.

3. A new or unique product. Also a distinct advantage if your product has the essential elements outlined above. Remember though, that old products come back around too.

4. Product has retail sales potential. A big advantage, as a strong promoter will have an eye on the huge sales that can be made through retail sales.

5. Repeat sales or continuity program. Does your product get used and need replacing? Let's say it's a polish – ready to be positioned for retail sales. Is there a continuity of items that can be provided on a regular basis? Maybe like a record collection or a how to course. Once again, this is not essential but an added advantage.

6. Is there potential for a well-known person to be a spokesperson? Sometimes this can be an advantage but the person should be a good "fit" with the product. Also, remember that the product is the real "star" so attention should not be diverted from it.

7. Testimonials. These can be regular people or celebrities. If they are celebrities who can speak with authority about the product this can be interesting. However, regular users of the item who can speak with some passion and conviction can be a strong advantage in a TV spot.

Categories of Direct Response TV Products

Housewares & Home Appliances
Kitchen and Cooking Products
Hardware
Tools
DIY
Craft Items
Automobile Items
Demonstration Items
Cleaners
Sleeping Helpers (including mattresses and toppers)
Fitness and Slimming Products
Beauty and Look Good Categories
Weight Loss
Skin Care & Beauty
Pain Relief
Vitamins and Supplements
Motivational & Self Improvement Tapes, Discs and Books
Business Opportunities
Hobby Products
Musical Compilations
Collectibles
Heritage and Ancestry

Listen, Learn, Watch and Improve

OK - you're just starting out and good luck to you because if you hit on a winner "overnight" that will be terrific. On the other hand, like any profession, there are skills to be learned - work at it and you can only get better. As you look for products, go back and read through these pages many times so you can get better at identifying and developing the right products and packages ("lump ups"). Watch the masters – those folks running successful products on TV. Follow them on the Internet – look for blogs and info pages. Watch the experts on TV shows. Look at how these masters pick winning products – but also take note of their losers. If you see a product on TV for a short period of time and then it disappears, it was probably on test and didn't make it. What did they miss? Did they go against their better judgment and stray from the elements that are essential to a winning TV product? Discipline yourself to focus and stick with these winning elements. By understanding why bad picks did not succeed you can avoid losers – and that can be clever too. Watch the TV shopping channels to see what items win. But also analyze the losers – ask yourself why they failed. Try to work out as much as possible on paper before spending money on a product. Many times you can win or lose on the "drawing board" so to speak. Work your product, on paper, through the necessary elements – be thorough and logical. When you are researching a product you'll want to learn as much as you can about it and you will – because, in a very natural way, that is really automatic. Have you ever noticed that when you become interested in a particular subject you keep seeing and hearing points related to it? I find that the more I positively concentrate on a subject - be it product or whatever - then more and more information comes my way that is related. Some people refer to this as "teachers" helping you, some call it "messages" coming your way - I've even heard it called "mind programming" when you concentrate on these thoughts. I do know that it happens. Work at it, be positive, be alert, be aware and know that it is within your control to learn, to improve and to get better.

Here's a tip you can use:

1. Write down your goals.

2. Figure out ways to achieve them.

3. Work on these goals, in some way, every single day.

Selling Concepts – the Hook to Make it Happen

Always remember that sometimes a seemingly ordinary product can be turned it into a million dollar seller by hooking on to a clever selling concept. A cookware set is a regular store shelf item – but the Armourcote Cookware became something special.

What can you say about a kitchen knife to make it into a unique item? How about calling it the Ginsu Knife and giving it a Japanese image of sharpness - complete with the mystique of the Orient?

This approach can help if you find an old TV product – maybe from 10 or 20 years ago – and, with a clever selling concept, you can bring it to life all over again.

Watch TV

You should also watch TV spots for demo products. This can teach you how to construct a demonstration for items that don't already have one. Watch how the demonstrations relate to the products. Get an understanding of how a good TV product needs to solve a problem – a big one. Study the elements of the TV spot demonstration and its sequence. Use a dramatic benefit – the major benefit - early in the demonstration you construct. It is from the demonstration that the TV spot is created. What may have started as a live pitch (demonstration) of 5, 10 or 15 minutes is reduced, with its essence effectively captured, to a 2 minute or 60 second TV spot. You'll notice that even "long form" infomercials have these "short form" TV spots in them. The full demonstration may be in the infomercial – but it's the shorter spot that drives home the points and makes the sales.

Developing the "Magic Factor"

You have read, above, about what I call the "Magic Factor". Let me repeat and emphasize this point. If you are working on a demonstration for a product just ask yourself this; "If I had the ultimate power what would I make this product do?"

Then see if the product can do it. That's how you find the most dramatic elements of a demonstration. Just use your own imagination to create something that is, at the same time, logical. You need something really dramatic to make a point to the folks who live in this "I've seen it all before" age.

Be blatant so you don't leave people guessing or unsure of the point you are making. How about cracking a nut with a steamroller, or even a sledgehammer, to show it can be done easier with your new "Miracle Nutcracker" – would this get attention?

A famous demo from times gone by was the guy with a hard hat glued to a metal girder – the glue was strong enough to hold him aloft. This demonstrated the strength of the glue.

An egg swirling round in a frying pan shows how non-stick the surface is.

Chopping wood, or cutting through quartz, with a kitchen knife may seem a bit way out – but when the knife cuts thin slices from a tomato it makes the point as to just how sharp the blade is. Even rough treatment didn't dull the blade and it's still "sharp enough to slice a tomato wafer thin". Think up a demo that makes a dramatic point visually and is easy to understand in a few seconds.

Now for my big secret....

My own "Million Dollar" secret!

This is the unveiling of a very special secret. But, be aware that you need to read all that I have written, in all these pages, in order to fully understand what you need to do to take advantage of this secret. At the time it was a unique recipe that I formulated to develop TV product packages and create some of my best sellers of all time. It has been proven by results many times over.

The Lump Up

To create a dramatic winning package certain elements should be present – it's like a recipe for success – and here it is:

The Star:
A "star" product containing all that I refer to in the "necessary" list shown above. Note that this must be a demonstration item.

The Pile Up:
A multiple set or kit. Say, 6,10 or 12 pieces – like a screwdriver set. You don't need to demonstrate this, just lay it out so it looks like a lot. I call this a "pile up".

The Supporting Bonus:
A "supporting bonus" item, which must also be a demonstration product. This should be in the same category so, if the "star" is a tool, the supporting item should be a tool – a kitchen item goes with a

kitchen item, and so on. The supporting item is usually brought on as a bonus at (or near) the end of the TV spot. Sometimes it can be shown right after the "star" product.

The Sweetener:
This is a possible addition. A "sweetener" can possibly include some information – a book or a disc – with the package. This gives it a bit of "window dressing" and you can get "good mileage" for an inexpensive piece.

And, this is the huge secret – the biggest one of all!

I created this concept way back when I was developing packages for sale by demonstrations. In those days it became known as the "lump up". The real secret is that all components in the package must complement each other – they must flow and "make music" together. Just like the members of a dynamic team, they ALL have to work together. Here is an additional secret – a secret that needs a special understanding to go with it – you need the gut feeling that leads you in the right direction to show how to put the pieces together. You may have this talent naturally or you may need to develop it by exposing your mind to products and demonstrations - many times this skill can be developed and I hope what I have written helps you in that development - but, like a discriminating collector, always keep your focus on the plan you have written down.

Please, also, read everything that I have written, in all these pages, to fully understand all you need to do to use, and take advantage of, my "Million Dollar" secret and bring forth your own creation in a dramatic and dynamic way.

Example Packages:

Shur-Lok Wrench Kit:

STAR:
Shur-Lok Wrench
Big-Lok Wrench (larger size)

PILE UP:
10 Piece Screwdriver Set

SUPPORTING BONUS:
Pocket Tool Kit – glass & tile cutter that also stripped wire and sharpened knives

Chinese Wok Set:

STAR:
Wok
Cooking Ring
Domed Wok Cover

PILE UP:
Tempura Rack
Strainer
Spatula
Rice Paddle
10 Pairs of Chopsticks

SUPPORTING BONUS:

Bamboo Chinese Steamer and Cover

SWEETENER: Book on Wok Cooking

That's it folks, after many years of using my methods to create several fortunes I'm giving my GREATEST SECRETS to you. I sincerely, and earnestly, hope that you make a fortune from what I have shown you.

Write a note to let me know how you get on. My E Mail is:
Michael@MichaelWalshe.com

Read more about the author in the following......

Some highlights from the author's career...

Knowing history will help you imagine the future and always remember that the future starts in the present time..... Michael Walshe

Being a marketer and a historian may seem an unlikely combination but nevertheless this is Michael Walshe's lot in life. Going down both roads has meant a life filled with excitement, the constant thrill of the hunt and an understanding, from his historical studies, of the needs of regular folks. This he has gleaned through research of what they have endured and enjoyed throughout the ages. Walshe started in the business of Direct Response TV (DRTV) marketing way back in 1976 when he was an immigrant pioneer and innovator in the roots of the industry. Even before then, going back to over 45 years ago, his career relied on discovering and developing new products suitable for demonstration sales. Walshe "cut his teeth" in the world of merchandise as a pitchman demonstrating products that were on the "cutting edge" of new ideas. He recalls that this hands on work got him closer to understanding products than he could have by any other method of study. He learned what made the items tick, the problems they solved, and how to construct demonstrations to effectively sell them. This is why he has insisted on always being part of the "pitchman world" no matter what direction his work has taken him. His first big winner on TV was the Miracle Painter – an item better known for its catchy, attention grabbing opener of a man in a tuxedo painting a swirl ceiling. Obviously created to illustrate this DIY tool's resistance to dripping and splashing. This dynamic product was soon followed by the Armourcote Cookware TV spot. Its opening scene featured an egg dropping on a huge diamond with the words "some day this may be the world's hardest non stick surface - but you can't cook on a diamond." More winners came around that time, with the most memorable, in Walshe's greatest hits, being the world famous Ginsu Knife. People still remember the karate chop on a tomato – what an opening – over 30 years later. Slicing tomatoes, chopping wood and cutting cans, this TV spot set the standard, in marketing technique, for all that followed in the industry. It blazed its way, through TV screens, into living rooms across the nation to become a "never to be forgotten" American icon. It should be noted that Walshe and the legendary Arthur Schiff worked together on the Armourcote and Ginsu projects. It was then that they created the phrase "But wait there's more!" which continues to be used (in its original and variant forms) as a TV spot standard. Through the 80's Walshe had a string of winners with tools, gadgets, DIY marvels, and he was the first marketer to offer the Chinese Wok on TV. This was in a 2 minute commercial before the days of the 30 minute infomercial. He also created what is believed to be the first long form (30 minute) infomercial for sales of a product by a hands on pitch – a dynamic kitchen wizard called the Rap Tou. Long form infomercials were still fairly new and prior to this were mostly for real estate and money-making courses. The Rap Tou show put a real pitchman, Roland Babin, in front of the cameras. Walshe's strong point has always been in developing new products. But, more important in building what he calls "the package." This refers to the lineup of items and bonuses that go to making a winner. In line with this production he ties them into what he refers to as a "sales concept" - the overall premise on which a need for a product is based. All of this he weaves into a compelling script for a TV commercial. During the 90's and into the new millennium Walshe has been even more closely involved in the script writing and production side of the DRTV business. Two outstanding productions being the Rocket Chef and the Titanium II knife set. The former being a manual food processor - he took an already produced infomercial from being in red ink to make a huge success. Walshe later went on to turn this product into a major 2 for 1 offer. In those days he called it a "TWOFER" (2 for the price of 1) and now this approach is widely used and known as a "BOGO" (Buy 1 get 1 FREE). Always looking for new products and categories to apply TV marketing methods to, Walshe eventually merged his skills in marketing and his talents as an entrepreneur with his lifelong passion for history. He founded The Historical Research Center and set out on a quest to research every family name in the world and to supply a Family Name History to every family in the USA. Soon a team of dedicated researchers was compiling original histories by using individual research. The tremendous expense of doing this as a manual effort paid off when Walshe established a dealer network to sell Family Name Histories and Coats of Arms at shopping malls and high profile tourist locations around the world. These unique historical items are now available through TV marketing and the commercial uses the time honored approach as it dramatically tells viewers that the family name is "a precious legacy left as the means to keep your family united" – is that a great secret revealed? Does it highlight a problem needing to be solved? Think about it – are families spread out? The TV spot, featuring a backdrop of Ellis Island, landing point of ancestors to 100 million Americans, has been on TV screens far and wide. Walshe travels extensively and uses part of his time seeking new products and ideas. He believes that products and ideas are the lifeblood of modern economy.

Bonus Volume coming up – don't miss it....

Bonus Volume

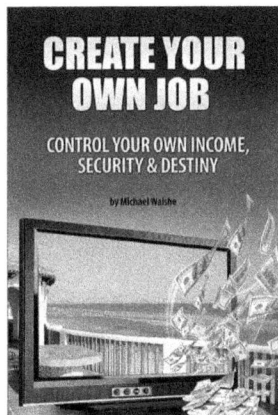

Create Your Own Job...

Control your own income, security & destiny

Create Your Own Job…..

Control your own income, security & destiny…..

The approach in "Create Your Own Job" is definitely a "think outside the box" concept. When people search for a job they usually focus on the use of their formal skills and qualifications. What they studied for – what they trained for. But we all have other aspects to our lives and may be as skilled or more skilled in other areas. Do you have hobbies, passions, experience from volunteer work, secondary studies, cultural influences? Even speaking with a different accent can bring opportunities your way.

In a moment we will examine each of these skills or knowledge banks to see how they can open up opportunities. But first let me share my belief that we must think from the ground up – put aside what you have done, used or relied on to give yourself work and an income.

Social influences, like what our Dads worked at or the predominant industry in our area, can have a profound effect on the career we chose in life. But many times we work purely to get a living not at what we enjoy. Why? But, more important, why not change this?

What I loved best at school is what I love best now – writing. For a while, other influences took me away from using this passion in my work – but eventually I returned to it. Do you have an earnest desire to change direction in your working life? It's easier than you think so read on if your answer is YES.

I am indebted to Alvin Toffler who said:

"If I had studied economics I would have been taught that the factors of production are land, labour and capital. ``Knowledge'' doesn't appear. Today, knowledge not only must appear in that list, it dominates the others. If you have the right knowledge at the right place at the right time, that means less labour, less energy, less capital, less raw materials and less time. All the other inputs of economic production for the conversion of natural elements into what we call wealth can be done far more effectively and efficiently through the application of knowledge."

He also said:

"We are talking about knowledge in a much broader sense. I don't mean just computer data, I also mean ideas. I think we use the word almost in a sense of culture. What's really interesting is that we believe the nature of technology and the nature of the economy will drive the nature of social change. Which makes us sound like technological determinists. However, it is the culture that increasingly drives the technology and the economy. The economy is based on knowledge and that is based on culture."

The approach that I am proposing relies on knowledge that you have within you. I am also asking you to blend your knowledge with ideas that can create your ideal job or business. That job may, in practice, be in employment for others or you may become self-employed in your own business.

Let's take an individual look at some skills or knowledge banks to see where your opportunities lie.

Hobbies:

Do you have a hobby that you could turn into a job or a business? Here's an actual event that happened recently and is one of the bright sparks of these tough economic times. A man in New Jersey was laid off from his job in the technology sector. Well, he needed to make a living and didn't want to sit around for long. His hobby, for many years, had been in do-it-yourself work – fixing up around the home. He believed that the skills he had learned placed him in a good position to offer handyman services in his local community. He also found there was a need for the services of a good handyman. A lot of this type of business comes from referrals – so, after some initial projects, a handyman can ask his clients for the names of friends and relatives who might want work doing. So here is a business that can be started, and sustained, with very little (if any) advertising – a business that, with a little help, can be self-promoting. Of course, if your hobby is also a passion you will not only do good work, you will also be able to sing the praises of your services with a vigor that captures attention very effectively.

Passions:

Do you have a passion for reading or music? If so, maybe you have a collection of books or records. Have you ever thought of dealing in books or music (or both) and building this as a business? Years ago this might not have been so easy. But now with eBay and craigslist, and many similar services, anyone can set up in the business of buying and selling. Your collection, providing you can bear to part with it for a greater good, now becomes an inventory of merchandise that is the basis for your business. As you sell you will be on the look out for similar items selling at prices lower than yours. So, you buy some to replenish your inventory. Buy and sell – sell and buy and all the time make sure the margin between buying and selling is in your favor to allow the profit percentage you have targeted. By the way, it is a good idea to write up a simple plan before you start. Layout your expectations and goals and this can act as your road map along the way. You can always tweak and change the plan but having it to refer to will give you the essential clarity required in business. One of the good things about having an online selling business is that you can do it part time and you can also involve other family members. So if you get another job you don't have to give up your business – you can continue to grow it. Build the business and build income for extras in life and to put away some "rainy day" money. Who knows, perhaps your online business can become your main source of income and even allow you to build wealth. This method of business is good in many ways. Number one, you can start at whatever level suits you – two, it can be applied to so many passions that people have. There are many more points in favor of it, including the independence this type of business can give you. Do you have some items of sports memorabilia? How about political memorabilia? Then there is jewelry – look at all the companies offering to buy your gold based on the value of its weight. Check out if you can get more by selling your pieces for their value as jewelry – and start your own business at the same time. Just go on eBay and do your research right there. All sorts of collectibles are being sold online. Go on eBay and scout around a little – you will soon see. Both eBay and Craigs List are easy to understand and you can be walked through all the setup procedures online. If you want to learn more there are books and discs available.

Volunteer Work:

This can be a terrific source of knowledge. Sometimes volunteers for a cause, such as a homeless shelter, are asked to take a fulltime position. In effect their volunteer work has allowed them to showcase their talents and somebody has decided they can use those talents. Now, you can also learn business skills by doing volunteer work in a particular category. I know of a couple who learned the event planning business by volunteering at a community festival. They went on to set up their own event planning business that also involved securing bookings for entertainers. If you volunteer for a charity, and use this as a chance to expose your skills and talents, you may get a chance to work full time for the charity. You may be able to secure work in businesses related to the charity. Thinking ambitiously, maybe you can work on research relating to a particular aspect of the charity and set up a vehicle to offer your own specialized services. But, here's a very important part, while you are volunteering you will have the chance to network with any number of people who work in different businesses and industries. You can gain knowledge and learn much from them and you can also prospect for work, either in an employed position or for your own business. Even volunteering you time to care for elderly people can introduce you to an area where you can use your skills. There are so many people who need to have elderly relatives cared for in a skilled and compassionate manner.

Secondary Studies:

Here I refer to subjects you learned at school, or later in life, that you did not use or follow in order to pursue your career to date. How about your study of a second language? Could you improve these skills to a level where you could act as a translator or interpreter? Both services are in big demand and these are skills that you could use in a self-employed capacity. What do you know of sports? Were you on one of the school teams? Now come outside the box and ask could your love of the sport get you work in its administration area? Maybe in coaching or refereeing. How about selling sports related products? Here is an area you may find lucrative and enjoyable. Did you learn sewing? Do you know how many people have a need for these services – in dressmaking, alterations work and so on. Set yourself up to do this work in your neighborhood and it can fall into the same pattern as the handyman business. Good work can serve to get referrals and you could go from strength to strength. Can you do simple accounts? How about offering bookkeeping services to small businesses in your area? Did you study art at school? Maybe you can bring your knowledge up to date and buy and sell art on eBay. If so, pick a niche specialty that is in line with your knowledge and suits you – what you enjoy. How many people study metal work, woodwork, or in the auto shop at school, and then go on to pay dearly for these services while working to make that money in another career? If you enjoy these functions you can make a job or a business from them – for all are in demand. There may be many other trades you have gained a knowledge of and you may not start work as an expert, but you can many times assist and learn more on the job.

Natural Skills:

Do you enjoy cleaning house? Many people make a fabulous living at offering this service around their town. Once again, do good work and you will get valuable referrals. How about gardening? A fabulous business to set yourself up in. There is always a demand for lawn service and gardening. Many people don't realize that their rudimentary computer skills can, with a little development, be used to teach others. Many have to do a full college course to learn all about computers, their history, hardware, software, bits and bites – all to formally enter the workforce in this field. How many years did all that take, and how much of it do people use in their own jobs? Would you like to hear of a shortcut to a business in computer software teaching? Don't set out to be the be all and everything to the computer industry but just focus on one, maybe two or three, specialties. Set yourself up as an expert in Windows or Word in very short order. You can now learn these skills in a very short time, by training with either manuals or discs. There are many people who have a mental block on using those same manuals and discs and would much prefer to be walked through the learning process by a skilled and friendly teacher. Are you a competent typist? With the number of computers in use there are tons of people who would like to type proficiently rather than using the two-fingered version many employ.

Cultural Influences:

Have you been immersed, perhaps all your life, in family culture and the culture of your ancestral group? Do you have a passion for history, genealogy, ancestry, or family lore and stories? If so, you may be a candidate to run a Historical Research Center business. I founded this, over 20 years ago, and I am still very much involved with it. The Historical Research Center, Inc (or HRC as it is known) has built up databases of Family Name Histories and Coats of Arms. All are individually, and originally, created and not the generic type seen on some websites. Approved dealers are licensed to use these databases and the skills and knowledge can be passed on to enable you to set up in the business of supplying some very appealing, and much desired, gifts that people then treasure as heirlooms. It really is quite simple and people take to this business very quickly. I have included some information in this volume, and have available a demo program to show a sampling of family name histories and coats of arms - and how you can access this data on your computer – this demo can be sent to you on request. These family name histories and coats of arms cover countries around the world just to show you the scope. But, HRC has a library of rare books, documents, manuscripts, and databases that allows researchers to study millions of family names. Just so this doesn't sound like it's just an advertisement, I go back to the premise of using your skills and knowledge. If your own can lend themselves to this work it can be more than just a job. You can build a business that you can make lucrative. Many HRC business owners have other family members involved and this, too, can be very satisfying.

Accent as an Advantage:

It is quite amazing to think of the number of skills, talents, gifts and knowledge that can help to nail down a good job or get you into your own business. Many times we think of these in another section of our lives. That is why it is essential to "step outside the box" and shift the pieces around a little. Even the way you speak, something you've grown up with, can be an advantage. A friend of mine got a job, recently in these tough times, just because he has an accent from a European country. The company was looking for people to be on the phones taking customer service calls from customers in Europe. They wanted them to be able to talk to people they could more easily relate to. By the way, my friend got this job through networking when a pal pointed him in the right direction. You never know what can bring an opportunity your way – so always be sure to keep an open mind.

No End to the Talents You Can Use

There are so many talents, skills and banks of knowledge that you can use to create a job or start your very own business. Just follow this guide:

1. Make a list of your own talents.

2. Put them in order of those you enjoy most and so on down.

3. Figure out an idea of the number of people who could use these services. If it's a reasonable pool of would be clients (or employers) it will be worth pursuing.

4. Decide whether you want to use the chosen talents to seek a job or "Create Your Own Job" by starting a business. Bear in mind that a business can be started with one person – YOU.

5. Write a simple (short) outline plan – and go for it.

6. Remember, people will, most times help so never be shy about seeking help or advice from those around you. Even from other business owners in your community.

Building Business:

Even in this high tech age, one of the best ways to get new business, or seek a job, is by networking and creating awareness through word of mouth. These are also the least expensive forms of promotion – so don't neglect them. You can be your own best advertisement and never forget this – the person behind the business is its best spokesperson, ask any car dealer. But also ask your friends and relatives about any openings for work, your services, and your business. Do not be shy about it. After all, what are friends for if they can't give you a little help? But, do not forget to give the help back when it's needed. Better still, you can be the first one to give the help. The bottom line is that anyone you know can be a source of putting you in touch with work or business. Even former employers, or workmates, can help – perhaps even more so. You never know what others know and, as the old saying goes, if you don't ask you won't get. Many jobs are found through networking and a huge number are never advertised.

More from Alvin Toffler:

I have learned a whole lot from this man – going right back to his book, Future Shock, which was published in the seventies. He claims he is not a predictor of the future – but a lot of what he wrote, along with his wife Heidi, has certainly come to pass. Here is short quote that is very pertinent to the matters you have just been reading:

"....like in real life, there is an enormous bank of knowledge in the community that we can tap into. So, why shouldn't a kid who's interested in mechanical things or engines or technology meet people from the community who do that kind of stuff, and who are excited about what they are doing and where it's going?....."

Why shouldn't you create your own livelihood by using the knowledge gained throughout your life? Why shouldn't you incorporate your ideas into your career? New ideas are the lifeblood of modern economy and your ideas can do more that create your own job – they can go on to create jobs for others too and you can see that lifeblood surging. Now that really is worth striving for.

And there's more….

While Your Mind is on Making Money

I think it is, so I'm going to repeat this - but it's well worth reading…..

While your mind is on making money here's a way to potentially make some fairly quickly. Think of it as a stepping-stone and a way to make some seed money that you can use to get into the TV product business – where the big money is. Perhaps it's a way to make a living while you are working at finding and developing TV products. In the meantime what's wrong with making a few hundred or even a $1,000 a week or more? Of course, this will depend on your own ability and how hard you go at it - but all work and business does. You're not afraid of trying hard are you? Anyway, if you take a look at the catalog of information below, and the demo program - which I can send to you (just e-mail me at the address below) - you will find all the details. It's about a ready-made business that others are making money at right now. The monetary investment is low and potential rewards are high. So, as long as you are prepared to invest your time, you can be on the first steps to your own fortune. I started in my own business, over 45 years ago, with start up money of about $25 – those were the days - I can honestly say that I've never looked back. This is something to think about but you may be in a position where you don't need help to get started – if so, that's OK.

However, if you are interested, see the catalog of information that I have included for you. Then get and review the demo program. Try out the demo features contained in it – and then give us a phone call or send an e-mail.

This is an ideal business for anyone who is bright and can hold a reasonable conversation. It can also get you out and about in the shows or shopping centers (malls) where you can be "in the swim of things" with lots of products all around you.

Another thing, it's a great opportunity for pitchmen who know how to present a product – and some may be reading this. Maybe those who are at the stage where they want to slow down a little and get off the box onto a wider platform. But, take note of what I said – "anyone who can hold a reasonable conversation" should take a look. By the way, you may want to do a favor for a friend or relative so, if the bonus volume is not for you, why not pass this info on to someone who may be looking for a job. **Then they can create their own job – and say thanks to you!**

My e-mail is: michael@michaelwalshe.com

UPDATE: I recently had the pleasure of some conversation with a man who could not get work after leaving college. He actually went to work for free and learned much about the business of video production. This man is now a partner in a huge advertising agency with TV commercials on nationwide TV – that's "CREATE YOUR OWN JOB" for sure.

See on the next pages for the catalog that I mentioned.

WHAT IS YOUR NAME?

You are linked to the past by your Family Name, which has been in existence for hundreds - perhaps over a thousand years. What is its origin? Was it taken from the Bible, a Clan name, the name of a village, an occupation, an ancient landmark?

Who were the people who proudly bore this fine family name? Were they nobility or royalty? Discoverers or adventurers? Innovators, artist or inventors? Military figures or political leaders? Rebels or pioneers? Community leaders or religious figures? Maybe famous citizens or early immigrants?

These mysteries can now be answered by The Historical Research Center. Compiled and presented in Family Name Histories which are works of literature in their own right. All originally and individually researched, the characters jump off the page at you and seem to come to life as a link with your own heritage. Our database reveals many facets to a particular family name, including the origin and meaning of the name, vital facts about people who carried it, events they were involved in, occupations they pursued, intriguing details and the earliest recorded date found. Plus, early immigrants and the Blazon of Arms describing heraldic markings, colors and designs.

These valuable databases can be used in your business to produce products that have a reputation for guaranteed authenticity.

Remember, everyone has a name... everyone can be your customer.

Remember too, the population is growing and is now over 300 million.... Many more potential customers !

CALL NOW FOR YOUR FREE CD. (800) 940.7991

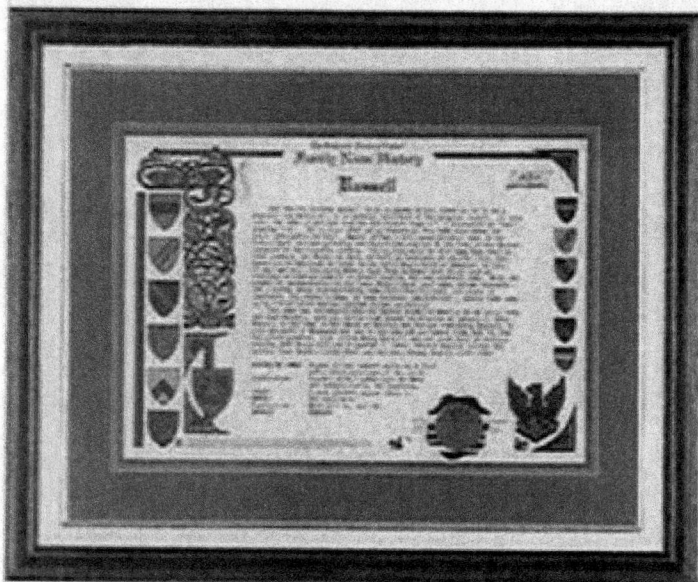

TESTIMONIALS

"I received the beautifully framed Coat of Arms and History of the Armistead name yesterday and am just delighted. It is beautiful and I can't thank you enough!"   - United States Senator Bill Armistead

"Just wanted to drop you a note to thank you for the beautiful job that you did on my recent order. This was a Christmas present for my Dad. He is the impossible-to-buy-for person. I do not normally see Dad very emotional, but when he opened the gift, tears came to his eyes. It was certainly beautiful!
                                                                    - Joe Armor

"I appreciate your research historians undertaking the project of studying my family name and providing me with such interesting material. I will proudly display these items in my home."   - Head Coach Pat Riley

"Frank Sinatra asked me to thank you and the Historical Research Center for the Sinatra Family Name History. It was a wonderful gift – both Mr. and Mrs. Sinatra enjoyed reading the obviously well-researched document. The Coat of Arms was beautifully done and has a prominent place among Mr. Sinatra's most cherished mementos."   - Susan Reynolds

"Harrison Ford has asked me to thank you for the beautiful Coat of Arms and Family Name History....Mr. Ford likes it very much."   - Renee M. Willis

"Thank you for .... the beautiful authentic Coat of Arms Marino Family Crest."
                                                                    - Dan Marino

Thank you for...My Coat of Arms and Family Name History. - Sharon Stone

"I am so happy that I ordered my Family Coat of Arms. Your company did an outstanding job and I can't wait to hang it proudly in my home."
                                                                    - Suzanne Moore

"It's a touch of elegance that is just timeless....   It really is a signature that no one else has."   .... Customer quoted in USA Today

Some Happy Customers you may have heard of .....

Why Start An "Is Your Name Here" Dealership

1. **Turnkey Operation:** Immediate Cash Flow

2. **Versatility:** Wherever you can plug in a computer you can sell products i.e. - Malls, Fairs, Conventions or even from your home.

3. **Unique Product Line:** The Historical Research Center is the leader in this unique area. Basically there is no serious competition!

4. **High Profit Margins:** Easily managed inventory combined with high demand provide great margins.

5. **Easy to Use:** Simply select the name, select the product then print.

6. **Corporate Support:** Customer Service, Product Development...We are here for you.

7. **Investment in our products:** Enough saleable inventory to generate over $6,800 in retail sales.

8. **Low Inventory Cost:** Inventory consists of customized heritage items, scrolls and computer uses to make valuable products. Customized items are drop shipped to the customers. You get the money up front.

9. **Small Initial Investment:** For just $995 you get inventory, assorted products and license to software to produce products.

10. **Special Mall Pricing:** Discounted cost of goods pricing is available for cart and kiosk operators.

Potential Profit Examples

Weekly Sales	$1,995.00	$2,995.00	$3,990.00
Cost of Goods	$480.00	$721.00	$960.00
Gross Profit	$1,515.00	$2,274.00	$3,030.00

These are some examples based on selling only Family Name Histories and using our regular cost of goods pricing. Your own efforts and the product mix you choose to sell can vary your results - you have control.

An average take of $9,000 a week keeps me very happy plus I really enjoy this profession too.

The business is unique and its versatility is a plus.
Right now I'm looking for more sales locations. The Historical Research Center is a great company to deal with and I never have a need that's not catered for."
John Brett – Los Angeles, CA

Here's a toast to coat-of-arms popularity "Manufacturers and artists are being bombarded with commissions for items bearing new or historical family crests. Some have started waiting lists and turned on their answering machines because of high demand....." .... USA Today

A FEW WORDS FROM OUR FOUNDER ....

My family has been involved in the study and discussion of heritage, families and family lore, the fascinating stories we are all linked to, for close to 200 years. To us, family lore is as important as the family tree and extends beyond the immediate family by exploring the meaning and origin of the family name. Going way back in time to understand how the family's treasured name came about in ancient times or during the medieval era.

In time, this prompted a quest to research as many family name histories and historical coats of arms as may be possible. The databases created as part of this venture have been the basis for producing products that have made many businesses successful and many owners secure and happy. I hope you will become part of this success story. Our library of books dating back to the 1600's and manuscripts and documents from earlier centuries, all used to collect information about people in history who bore our family names and facts about them, is here to continue researching family names for your customers.

Your involvement will contribute to the continuation of our work and any time you want my input you only have to ask.

Mick Walshe
Founder of The Historical Research Center

CURRENT PROMOTION FREE WEBSITE
FOR NEW BUSINESS OWNERS

The following pages are for your notes: